The French Selection

Arthur Eperon is one of the most experienced and best known travel writers in Europe. Since leaving the RAF in 1945 he has worked as a journalist in various capacities, often involving travel. He has concentrated on travel writing for the past twenty years and contributed to many publications including *The Times*, *Daily Telegraph*, *New York Times*, *Woman's Own*, *Popular Motoring* and the *TV Times*. He has appeared on radio and television and for five years was closely involved in Thames Television's programme *Wish you were here*. He has an intimate and extensive knowledge of France and its food and wine, as a result of innumerable visits there over the last forty years. In 1974 he won the Prix des Provinces de France, the annual French award for travel writing.

THE FRENCH SELECTION

Arthur Eperon's Guide to the Best of French Hotels

Foreword by Frank Bough

Photographs by Anne Conway

Pan Books/BBC

Also by Arthur Eperon
in Pan Books

Travellers' France
Travellers' Italy
(in association with the BBC)
Travellers' Britain
(in association
with the BBC)
Encore Travellers' France
Le Weekend

First published 1984 by
Pan Books Ltd,
Cavaye Place, London SW10 9PG
and the
British Broadcasting Corporation,
35 Marylebone High Street,
London W1M 4AA
9 8 7 6 5 4 3 2
© Arthur Eperon 1984
Foreword © Frank Bough 1984
Photographs © Anne Conway 1984
Drawings © Sue Dray 1984
Maps by Ken Smith
Art direction by George Daulby
Designed by Peter Holroyd
Photoset by
Parker Typesetting Service, Leicester
Printed in Spain by
Mateu Cromo Artes Graficas S.A.,
Madrid
ISBN 0 330 28630 7 (Pan)
ISBN 0 563 20362 5 (BBC)

THE SELECTION

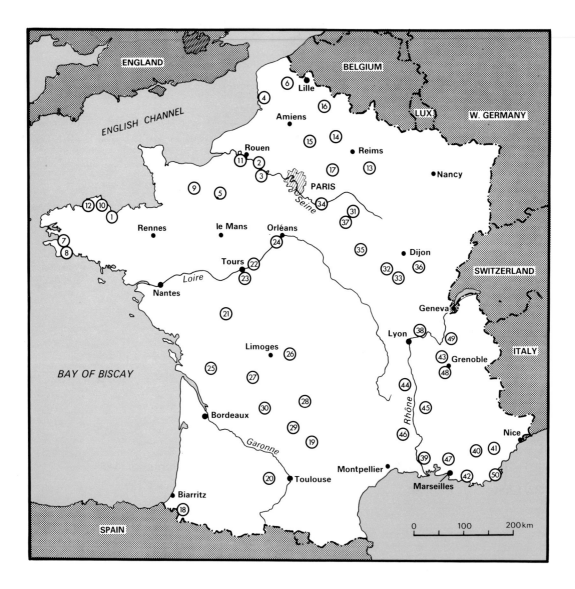

FOREWORD

Ever since Nesta and I made a series of films for BBC Television's *Holiday Programme* on Arthur Eperon's admirable *Travellers' France*, people have constantly asked us – Who is Arthur Eperon? Well, we both remember so well the first evening we met him. Tom Savage, the *Holiday Programme* Editor, had engaged us to follow one of Arthur's suggested routes through France. It was a typical BBC economy job. I did *Nationwide* on a Tuesday night, we travelled to Dover that evening, started filming at Dover docks on Wednesday morning, and the following Wednesday morning we flew back from Perpignan in time for me to do that evening's *Nationwide*, and pick up my more regular BBC schedule. Because the films were dotted through several weeks of the *Holiday Programme* the following winter, viewers thought we had spent months eating and carousing our way through France at their expense.

'How dare you fund the Boughs' holidays on the licence payers' money?' wrote one angry correspondent. A holiday? Nothing could be further from the truth. We'd decide on a location, quickly work out a few words and a treatment, amble nonchalantly through the shot: 'The food here is great, immensely reasonable, the wine is exceedingly drinkable, the lodgings cheap, and the view sensational.' Wander out of shot, dive into a small car and head for our next selection.

'The food here is even better, a little more expensive, the wine . . . the lodgings . . . the view even better . . .' – and so on, thundering through La Belle France far too quickly for our own health. And if you thought those long leisurely lunches, taken in the sylvan French countryside were a great self-indulgence, let me tell you that by the time you've persuaded the French waiters to take a route through the tables that favours the camera, persuaded the other guests not to gawp, and remembered your lines, the soup is cold, the chips soggy, and the tarte aux fraises savaged by the local wasps. Six days it took to shoot the whole lot, and if you really thought we were on holiday, then we're delighted, because that's exactly the impression we intended.

It was on that first Tuesday night that we met him. We'd just booked into the Dover Holiday Inn, where director, camera crew, us, and the author were to meet. He approached us enthusiastically, glass in hand (evaluating the quality of the Holiday Inn's cellar, I thought instinctively), his pear-shaped figure a glowing testimony to the diligence with which he had researched French cuisine on the world's behalf. That evening he became an admirable travelling companion – Arthur, as you know, is never going anywhere, just travelling – and a very useful one too, as we flogged our way down his route to Monsullon on the Mediterranean.

'Arthur! Where the hell are we now? What can I possibly say about this place?'

'Fontevrault, my boy – come over here. Did you know that this is where Richard the Lionheart, King of England is buried?'

'Arthur! Albi. What's so special about Albi?'

'Frank, my boy – bet you've got a Toulouse Lautrec print somewhere in your house,

probably in the loo. Let me show you the original, and his cane, and his top hat, and all those other lovely drawings and paintings he did of Paris and the Moulin Rouge.'

He never failed me. Well, as I write this foreword, we're about to drive into France again, clutching at the coat-tails of Eperon once more, as he leads us enthusiastically through his latest definitive study of the gastronomic and alcoholic joys of that country – the very best he knows, his *French Selection*.

We haven't seen him recently. He's been researching meticulously we're told, and consequently, is more pear-shaped than ever.

We look forward with great delight to renewing the acquaintance of a lovely man, and fondly hope that you will enjoy reading this book during the winter nights, and watching our films of Arthur's *French Selection*, in the *Holiday Programme* in the New Year. Happy Travelling.

Frank and Nesta Bough,
Autumn 1984

INTRODUCTION

Years ago in *The Times* I described a well-known chain of hotels as 'cabinets for filing people away for the night'. I had a scolding letter, signed with a name something like 'Silas J. Brikbatter Jnr, Vice-President Public Relations', implying that I was an English yobbo who did not appreciate the finer things of modern civilization, like hot-drink dispensers, laundry lists for ordering breakfast, and closed-circuit TV. I was even cut off for four whole years from the company's handouts telling me glad tidings, such as Mario Sebastian Kelly had been appointed manager of the new hotel in Strollalong, Kentucky (with Mr Kelly's picture, looking dynamic). I am sorry if my readers felt deprived.

Since then, I have found how useful these look-alike hotels can be to prevent that travelling feeling, especially if I have to be at Heathrow at 6.30a.m. to catch a plane, or if I am staying up half the night in New York, London or Cannes while other men dance with my wife and I want to sleep undisturbed until 10a.m. But even on business in big cities, I like to drive out to a hotel with real fresh air instead of recycled conditioned air, a view of the country beyond the building alongside, and where the patronne is in the entrance hall and the patron in the kitchen or vice-versa.

Big hotel chains have not made much headway in France. The French like individuality. So do I.

So the fifty hotels which I have chosen are all very individual. They are *not* necessarily among the most luxurious and efficient hotels I know, with gastronomic meals, perfect wine lists and polished service. Those would have been nearly all members of the Relais et Châteaux Hôtels de France organization.

I have chosen the hotels because I like them. They all have comfort, good cooking and interesting wines. Most are in beautiful surroundings, though some are chosen as good touring centres and others as attractive hideouts

from big cities. I have gone for value.

All have a special atmosphere and friendly people running them. You may well be asking why I chose to write such a personalized choice in the first place. The answer is that so many people wrote and asked me to do so. After reading my two books *Travellers' France* and *Encore Travellers' France*, leaning heavily towards two-star Logis de France type hotels, and *Le Weekend* suggesting all sorts of hotels within a short run of ferry ports, a lot of people said: 'We are really looking for something a bit *better* . . .

something unusual. We don't mind paying a bit more for it.'

Barbara and I started with a list of 140 which we knew, or which had been recommended to us. We stayed and ate at all of them, some for the first time, some for the fortieth year in succession. At least eighty of them were very rewarding and seemed to deserve to be put in the book. I am sorry that we had to leave out many good ones, some run by my friends. Some were left out because a neighbouring hotel a few miles away was slightly more interesting or had slightly better food or better views.

Even after forty years of

travelling France, I am still entranced by the beautiful scenery. France is such a spacious land. Houses, traffic, pylons and factories do not intrude on the scenery so much as in Britain.

I have sought good regional cooking of fine fresh local ingredients and interesting regional wines. Regional dishes are becoming more difficult to find. Nouvelle Cuisine should, if nothing else, be inventive, but it is tending to make some dishes the same in Nouvelle kitchens all over France. As one chef told me very recently: 'Many younger people interested in food but not knowing much about it follow the Nouvelle fashion slavishly. They walk in here with the *Gault Millau* guide under their arm and consult it with the menu. It pays to have one or two of the standard Nouvelle dishes on the card to keep them happy.'

As I have said before, I have never claimed to be a gourmet – just one of the 'world's greatest consumers', as the Royal Automobile Club called me when I was writing their wine articles. I am still glad to call myself an experienced consumer rather than an expert. I should hate to have to spoil every meal by analysing it, just as I could never be a Master of Wine because I refuse to play mouthwash games with a sip and spit it out again. To assess a wine, I drink a bottle. I should truly hate to ruin my enjoyment of a meal because it was not technically 'balanced' or 'sufficiently light'. It is a pity that fashion has crept into cooking and tried to take over. I should adore to invent a totally new dish, but not just to add grapefruit to steak, mint to scrambled eggs, or replace cider, which has served duck so well over centuries, with raspberry or blackcurrant juice. The new should not replace traditional and regional cooking but complement it. Fashion brings snobbery and high prices for anything that is different, irrespective of quality. The French reputation for giving the best value in the world as well as the highest quality in their meals is severely threatened by the fashion for pretty patterns on the plate rather than offering satisfying fresh ingredients beautifully cooked.

At times I resent very strongly being offered lazy-chef's dishes like semi-raw duck's breast in raspberry vinegar with three slices of carrot and one potato instead of classic and regional dishes. As Peter Ustinov said about a production of *Don Giovanni*: 'When the mentality of smartness, of vogue, grips an authentic masterpiece, we have a right to rebel.' I am in full rebellion against the disappearance of delicious fresh French vegetables from many tables. I do not want six French beans making a pretty-coloured pattern with slivers of carrot. I want a plateful of beans – as a separate course if necessary. The duck should surely replace the cockerel as the French national symbol.

Regional wines are more popular. About twenty years ago when American and Japanese buyers started to force Burgundy prices beyond the reach of many French people, and under the EEC policy the Italians were undercutting the French on good plonk, the French ministry helped many vineyards in less-fashionable wine areas to grub out old types of vines producing rather mediocre wine, to replant and to improve their methods of viniculture. The results are really showing now. Wines like Cahors which had slipped back badly over many years have improved remarkably. Areas which were producing battery acid are now offering very drinkable wines. They are well worth trying. You will not, of course, find a Côtes de Buzet in the same class as a *grand cru* St Emilion, but still highly drinkable at a third of the price.

Noticeable differences between the three- and four-star hotels in this selection and the majority of one- and two-star hotels in *Travellers' France* are in the bedrooms and breakfast. The bedrooms of these fifty hotels are nearly all in excellent taste, with fine old furniture and delightful décor, not to mention excellent bathrooms. But why are so many loo seats made of frail plastic? I get quite twitchy as I sit on them. Nor have breakfasts deteriorated quite so much as in many cheaper hotels where slices of stale bread passed quickly under a grill have replaced croissants

and fresh bread. Some of the breakfasts in these selected hotels are a delight and nearly twice as dear as in the Logis-type hotel. Others are much the same price and much better. But even the best often serve hard, cold croissants. There is no excuse for this. If the hotel does not bake its own fresh at least someone can put croissants in a plastic bag in the deep-freeze when newly baked and heat them in the morning under a grill. This is one place where the deep-freeze does score. They taste almost like freshly-baked croissants.

Inflation has hit the cheapest menus in many hotels and restaurants and it is really much better value to pay a bit more for the middle-priced menus. Many of the cheap weekday menus offer little or no choice and are not my sort of meal at all. I do not like tripe, I think that tough contre-fillet beef is better braised than grilled, and I am against that sausage made of coarsely-cut guts called andouillette. I took one home and my dogs would not eat it.

Although inflation has hit all French meal prices, they are still usually the best value in the world. We became so used to getting bargains in France that some people I know really jib at paying £12 to 15 for a superb five-course meal when they would have to pay the same for three courses of inferior cooking at most establishments of the same class in Britain.

I do think that some, but not all, of the better French hotels and restaurants are pushing

their luck on wine prices. All right, we know about overheads and short seasons, but we also know the retail price of wine in France, which they do not even have to pay. A 400 per cent mark up is too much. One hotel keeper has reduced his prices as he found that his customers were simply drinking much less or picking the house wine, and the hotel was losing out.

Half-board terms are usually for three days or more and you are often given a special *pensionaires* menu with few choices. Room prices are still most reasonable compared with most other countries, even at luxury hotels.

The French people staying in the hotels I have chosen are usually very relaxed, *très gentil* and *correct* in their manners, which is still more important in France than elsewhere, but informal in their dress. They do not hurry the waiters or receptionist, they wait to be ushered to their table instead of picking the one they like best, which is what many of the British do, and if they are left with the menu for a long time before their order is taken they regard this as a compliment. The waiter must think they are *sérieux* about food. To be *sérieux* is also still important. I have heard many a light-hearted joking Englishman dismissed with the verdict: '*Mais il n'est pas sérieux*'. If any groups are jolly and hearty and stay up very late drinking they are usually Belgian – or British. I am not suggesting that the hotels are dull or I should not like them. They are

relaxed, calm but still friendly.

The French in hotels of this type used to be very formal in their dress, especially in the dining room. That has changed. There is a strange mixture of clothes in many hotels. I have seen a girl in a lovely cocktail dress dining with a man in jeans, a tweed sports jacket and open-necked shirt, and a man in a neat formal suit at table with another in shirt sleeves with no tie or jacket. They are on holiday, if only for the weekend, they are relaxing and they wear what they fancy. A girl may want to show off a fashionable new gown but her escort is not committed to dressing formally simply because she is.

An urbane, perfectly dressed, suave owner of one of the most beautiful of these hotels said to me: 'The only rule we ask of our guests is that they should not come straight from the swimming pool to the dining room in beach or swim wear.'

'Not even topless?' I asked.

'Definitely not topless,' he said. After that he did not think that I was quite *sérieux*.

I hope that you will stay at some of my selected hotels and enjoy them as much as I do. I could happily spend a

fortnight at any one of them.

Even one night of dinner, bed and breakfast to break a journey or when you have business in a nearby town is very rewarding and adds a real bonus to your journey. I think that most of them will tempt you to go back.

Anne Conway's delightful pictures will help to show you just how tempting they are.

I have divided the book loosely into regions to make it easier to use. Recently-built motorways have changed the shape and face of France. True, most of them, like the old Routes Nationales, radiate from Paris. The Parisians believe that this is to help the poor, deprived people of the provinces to reach civilization, while the people of provincial towns believe that it is to allow the poor people of Paris to escape from their concrete, traffic-jammed prison to fresh air and a life of peace.

The effect of the motorways has been to clear a lot of the older roads of heavy lorries and hurrying cars and to make it quicker and easier to reach many of the remoter parts of France, like the Auvergne, Ardèche, Les Landes, Savoy and Gascony, and the pleasant hotels hidden away in them. Yet paradoxically, although many of these hotels are within a few miles of the motorways, they are not so full now because of the modern urge to belt as fast as possible from city to city or to the coast without stopping or seeing anything. The hideouts I have chosen for this selection are not really for motorway belters. They are for people who regard the beauties of France as something to be savoured, just as much as the food, wine, and atmosphere.

A few years back, I should never have put Brittany, Normandy and the Pas de Calais in the same section. Brittany was a world apart, more of a separate country than Wales is to England. But the motorways to Rennes and Nantes have brought Southern Brittany close to Paris and the motorway from Rouen to Caen has brought not only Paris but Dieppe and even Boulogne to within a reasonable drive from those once-remote, lush and delightful areas of Normandy – Calvados and Orne – and almost to the doorstep of North Brittany.

The stretching of a motorway to St Omer, behind Calais and Boulogne, has brought those Channel ports much nearer to delightful areas like the Compiègne Forest, the lovely old medieval town of Laon, the Champagne wine towns and even Burgundy.

But unlike Britain, the French have not neglected

their other roads to build motorways. The smaller roads of France have improved enormously – better surfaces, better repair, and none of those jagged edges which were the curse of motoring in France at one time. Strange how we boasted for so long that our 'B' roads were the best in Europe, and now they are falling apart. When the economic crisis came, the French decided to invest in their roads to keep industry moving and the result shows already. But a lot of pretty and interesting villages and small towns have been by-passed, so more than ever it is worth taking time to explore. Don't just keep off the motorways – get on to the little 'white' roads. For that you need either the local 'yellow' *Michelin* maps or, better, the new *Michelin* Regional maps, numbers 230–245. They are the same scale as the yellow maps – 1cm to 2km – but cover up to three times the area, so you do not have to take so many and you save money. Number 230, for instance, covers the whole of Brittany. They are necessary in many cases to find the hotel I have picked and to follow the local drives which I have suggested. Fifteen of them cover the whole of France – and their detail goes right down to individual castles. Even some of my hotels are marked on them. Thank you , *Michelin* – you wouldn't like to put the rest on for me, would you?

Arthur Eperon

See inside back cover for key to room and menu grades, and credit card coding.

Book from the Book!

Reservations and bookings
for the hotels featured in this book,
and for cross-Channel ferries,
can be made on your behalf.
See inside back cover.

PAS
DE CALAIS/
NORMANDY/
BRITTANY

**Auberge du Manoir des Portes
La Poterie, 22400 Lamballe,
Côte du Nord (North Brittany)
(55km from St Malo; 2km
from Lamballe; on D768 from
Plançoët, turn left on D68 to
hamlet of La Poterie, through
village then right to Manoir).
Telephone: (96) 31.13.62.
Rooms D (single), E, F;
menus A (weekdays),
B (weekends),
D (shellfish).
Closed February; restaurant
Mondays, 1 September to 30
June.
Visa, Amex.**

A charming, warm auberge made skilfully from a fifteenth-century manor farm with a big courtyard. In open country 2km from the interesting, photogenic little hilltop town of Lamballe, it is hidden away in the hinterlands of North Brittany which are most attractive and worth exploring.

I found it one night about eight years ago and was a founder-guest. Even then, there was a warm welcome, with a woodfire burning in the dining room and flowers in the cosy bedroom which had a huge, angled beam running from the floor to the sloping wall and ceiling. Now more of the old building has been converted, including a cheerful and comfortable bar-lounge with another big stone open fireplace and more bedrooms, two with small balconies, in what was a *cellier* for making cider. All the bedrooms have private bathrooms and they are warm and cheerful, too.

It is a Relais du Silence, and a very friendly, intimate place to take a friendly, intimate partner. The courtyard which now has bright garden furniture under umbrellas, table tennis, and is floodlit at night.

There is a sauna. On the estate is a fishing lake, and swimming, tennis and horse riding are within 2km. It is a great spot for horse lovers. In Lamballe is a national stud of 150 stallions, mostly old-style post horses and Breton draught horses. You can see them go out every day, ridden or harnessed in tandem, pairs or fours. They are a magnificent sight. There is also a dressage school and a riding club, each with about forty horses. You can visit the stud on afternoons except in the covering season (mid-February to mid-July). The horse show is held the weekend after 15 August.

Lamballe has an important cattle and pig market. It is a pretty town of white houses above the river Guessant, with a Gothic church on a terrace looking down into the valley. The tourist office is in the fifteenth-century house of the executioner of those days. Executions were always a tourist attraction, anyway. Also in

 Dinan (32km) is the most photogenic place in Brittany. Its old houses and narrow streets are almost entirely enclosed by medieval walls. It stands 200 feet (60 metres) above the river Rance, with lovely views and a little port below. You can cross the river on a viaduct. It is a beautiful place to wander, browse and eat.

Pléneuf-Val-André (15km) is a seaside resort with three beaches of white sand, screened by green and rocky cliffs. A trick of the Gulf Stream makes the sea often warmer than in South Brittany. Pleasure boating port of Dahouët with sailing school.

Erquy (23km) – busy scallop fishing port; Caroual, with views of the bay, is best of several beaches. Moncontour (15km on D768) is an endearing little fortified town of granite on a spur above the meeting of two valleys. Alleys and stairs lead down to ramparts; the main square Place Penthièvre is of elegant eighteenth-century architecture. 5km before the town from Lamballe take D6 towards Collinée, right on D6A for Notre-Dame du Haut chapel (key from nearest farm) with statues of seven healer saints – St Livertin, clasping his temples like an advertisement on TV, cures headaches; so does Ste Eugénie; St Mamertin cures colic; St Léobin relieves rheumatism; St Méen heals sick minds; St Hubert is for sores and rabies, and Ste Houarniaule calms fears. But you must enter with a humble heart to get their help. Nearby is Touche-Trébry castle, which looks medieval but is sixteenth-century.

it is a museum of 4000 works of a local artist, Mathurin Meheut, including sketches made in the First World War which interest historians. The old castle was razed by Richelieu in 1626 because the Lord of Penthièvre, son of Henry IV and his mistress Gabrielle d'Estrées, conspired against him. The church is all that remains.

Food & Drink

Rightly, the Manoir has a good reputation for seafood, local and fresh, some from its own *vivier*. Its second menu offers eight grilled fines de clairs oysters from the *vivier* or a scallop salad, followed by grilled Breton lobsters (around 400 grammes) from the *vivier*, then sorbet à la poire William (a pear brandy), or charlotte aux fraises (a gâteau with whipped egg custard and cream, with strawberries). Not cheap, but when you remember the price of lobster everywhere, even in Brittany and Cornwall, these days, it is a bargain.

The weekday menu *is* cheap, especially as the main course choice is good. You start with a choice from a table of hors d'oeuvre). Then you can have pork chop with sauce Robert (onion sauce with mustard, vinegar and white wine which goes beautifully with pork) or flank of beef grilled with shallots or a choice of the chef's three or four dishes of the day, all with vegetables. On my last visit the chef's dishes were brochette of lamb grilled with a sweet and sour sauce, crayfish in sharp and rich Armoricaine

sauce, duck fillet with green peppers, or fillet of salmon trout grilled with almonds. Then there is a choice of dessert. It is one of the best value meals I have met in a hotel of this standard. On weekends it is a little dearer but you get a greater choice of hors d'oeuvre (quite a spread) and cheese as well as dessert.

There are some very tempting dishes on the card, too. The truffled chicken liver terrine made by the chef is delicious, the sliced kidney in sweet and sour cider sauce much better than we had expected, and the blanc de turbot à la moutarde ancienne absolutely delightful. Turbot is a strange fish. It can be very dull unless given the right sauce to accentuate its delicate flavour without overwhelming it. Chef Daniel Grogneuf braises the fish in the oven in wine and fish fumet (stock), takes the fish out and reduces the juices with crème fraîche (slightly sour cream), then adds mustard. It took Barbara, who does not like mustard, years to discover that in sauces it tastes quite different and enhances flavours without biting the throat that swallows it.

Gault Millau says that wine prices are too dear. I don't understand. They look cheaper to me than most other hotels of this calibre. True, only someone of the Rothschild set could afford 1000F for a bottle of 1971 Château Mouton Rothschild. But we had at a sixth of the price a 1979 Château du Tertre Margaux produced by the great Gasqueton family. It may only be a *cinquième cru*, a fifth growth, but so are some wines from Rothschild properties. Du

Tertre has the real Margaux bouquet and flavour of pricier wines, plus a lot of body, and the one Rothschild with whom I have wined and dined would not turn up his nose at it.

There are two good white wines at below average prices to drink with the shellfish – a very fruity Domaine de la Moussière Sancerre and Comte de Malestriot's Noé Muscadet sur lie. For a cheap red, do try 1981 Château Le Nègre from Côtes de Bourg. Bourg and Blaye wines of Bordeaux, from the right bank of the Gironde opposite Margaux and St Julian, are somewhat neglected in Britain, and in much of France. They are not up to St Emilion standards, for instance, but are very drinkable. Blaye wines are a bit lighter and fruitier, Bourg have more body. Both can be drunk young, but most Bourgs can be kept, though some people do not realize it. I have just finished a case of 1970 Guerry from Bourg and I swear that it was better than ten years ago and had still kept its Cabernet fruitiness, whatever the pundits say.

Hôtel de la Chaîne d'Or

La Chaîne d'Or
place St Sauveur,
Les Andelys, 27700 Eure.
Telephone: (32) 54.00.31.
Rooms B to F;
menus A, B, C.
Closed Monday evenings,
Tuesdays; January.

Like so many old French coaching inns, La Chaîne d'Or looks a bit run down from outside. As you drive into the courtyard you wonder a little if you should have come. You will be glad that you did.

There is nothing run down about the food or the service. The furnishings *are* old fashioned, befitting the old rooms. Most bedrooms are very big and pleasant. Some have two double beds, armchairs, settee, a table, and there is still room to dance. Some of the beds are enormous – an invitation to a romp. Bathrooms are new and excellent.

There are a few smaller double rooms – originally, no doubt, for servants of carriage customers. Not all have bathrooms, but they are fair value.

To get a room overlooking the Seine you would have to book ahead in spring or summer.

La Chaîne d'Or has one of the best positions on the Seine. It is on the river bank, looking across to an island where some rich man built a villa – now, alas, empty. On the far bank are trees and countryside, with an

old black-and-white Norman farmhouse by the water.

When Chaîne d'Or was built in 1751, a gigantic chain was suspended across the river to the island. Every passing boat had to pay a toll – 'droits de travers'. The inn was the paying office, and the locals made so much money from tolls that they called it the Chaîne d'Or – veritably a golden chain. Now Seine barges pass unhindered. The old fishermen's harbour has become a pleasure marina and there are boat trips on the river from June to September.

There are two towns. Petit Andelys by the river has narrow streets and a big square containing a plaque to Blanchard, first man to cross the Channel in a balloon and inventor of the parachute. The rest of Andelys, with an interesting church, half Flamboyant Gothic and half Renaissance, is grandly called Grand Andelys.

The ruins of Château Gaillard almost hang over the town. It was built in one year by Richard Lionheart of England

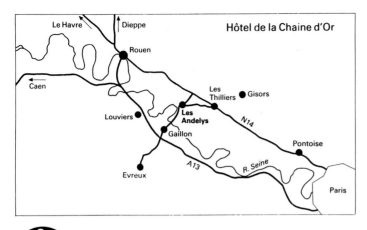

Hôtel de la Chaine d'Or

and Jean-Claude Foucault is a splendid host who serves personally in the dining room. His busy wife often helps, too. It is a local people's hotel. They drink in the bar and eat in the restaurant or in the separate bar-restaurant where you can get a good meal reasonably priced.

Food & Drink

The beamed dining room overlooks the river and has a big log fire burning in cooler weather. Service is helpful and so efficient that I have asked them to slow it down. I like to dawdle over good food. Alas, the French are convinced that all Britons are 'trying to catch the last train', as a French chef put it to me; hence the high-speed treatment.

Although the dearest menu has some slightly more interesting dishes, such as a delicious veal steak with mussels in light puff pastry, the middle-price menu is such good value that I would stick to it.

You could start with half-a-dozen oysters, but I would go for the salmon terrine which is one of the best I have eaten. It really tastes of salmon. So many are bland. It is served with a sauce Americaine not too sharp to spoil its flavour. The stuffed praires (small clams) are excellent, too – creamy and lightly grilled, not dry as they can be.

Duck or guinea fowl (pintadeau) in Calvados (apple spirit) are usually on the menu. Often farm duck is too tough in France, as it is often too dry in Britain. The Chaîne d'Or chef

LOCAL DRIVES Vernon (28km) and Giverny to see the house and gardens where the artist Claude Monet lived from 1883 until he died in 1926. A long, low, pink-and-green house bordering the D5E road, with beautifully restored gardens and a water garden with Japanese bridge and lily pond which Monet painted. (Open 1 April to 1 November, 10–12a.m., 2–6p.m.). From Les Andelys take Seine-side route with good river views to Tosney, Gaillon (15th-century castle was first Italian Renaissance building in Normandy); D316 across the Seine to D10, then D313 to Vernon (pleasant town striding the Seine). Return from Giverny on D5 along Epte valley, N114, left at Ecouis.

To Rouen by the Seine (55km) take the right bank route through Muids, Le Manoir, Belbeuf, Bonsecours – much more attractive than the other bank.

and Normandy to bar the route to Rouen. 'See my fine yearling,' he said, and while he lived Philippe Augustus of France dared not attack it. When weak King John reigned, the French took it. French soldiers got in through the latrines – the way we got out of Oflag XXIB in Poland in 1943. History insists that the latrine raid was led by a soldier called Bogis.

Later two queens were imprisoned there for sleeping with boy-friends – Blanche, wife of Charles IV, and Marguerite, wife of Louis X. Poor Marguerite was strangled. Such punishment for straying might lead to a national shortage of wives these days. Ironically the castle's name means 'happy or laughing'.

The views from the ruins are magnificent but the path is steep. You can drive round to a car park.

Even a short stay at La Chaîne d'Or gives you a different view of the Seine. Andelys is 94km from Paris, 39km from Rouen and a world apart from both.

The hotel is essentially French

makes a succulent dish with apples, cream and Calvados. I find it delightful.

The cheeseboard is outstanding, well chosen, fresh and good variety. As usual in Normandy, the hot apple tart with cream is a different dish from the apple tarts we have at home, made with eating apple varieties and so with much less sugar.

You could criticize the small choice on the main course — three dishes, usually of fish, fowl or game and meat. But everything is freshly cooked and in a menu at this price it is better to concentrate on a few fresh dishes.

The wine list has been chosen with much care. There is a good Muscadet sur lie to go with any of the three starters I mentioned, oysters, salmon terrine or clams. But there is also a highly-drinkable Sancerre at a low price these days, and it also comes in half-bottles. I have tried a very nice 1979 St Emilion Château Rochers Blanches with the duck, but if you are in a spending mood there is a fine Burgundy — 1976 Clos des Marconnets, from the vineyard at Savigny-les-Beaune which lost a lot of its land in the building of the A1 motorway but blessedly still produces a delightful wine: lighter, more delicate than some Beaune, with a lovely bouquet.

If you are in a saving mood, the Chaîne d'Or's house wine is no mouthwash and I like a glass with the cheese.

The atmosphere of the hotel (relaxed) and dining room (bustling and friendly), together with the river scene and the big bedrooms make the Chaîne d'Or delightful.

Château de la Corniche

**Château de la Corniche
Route de la Corniche,
Rolleboise,
78270 Bonnières-sur-Seine
(just off N13 between
Bonnières
and Mantes; leave A13
motorway
Rouen-Paris at Bonnières –
3km).
Telephone: (3) 093.21.24.
Rooms F–G (half-pension or
one meal a day must be
taken);
menus D, E, G;
half-board G
Closed 23 January to 10
March, also Sunday evenings,
Mondays from 1 September to
31 May.**

The bearded patriarch King Leopold II of Belgium, hard-headed businessman and high-flyer, built this folly last century in a magnificent hilltop position above a sweeping bend of the Seine, with terraced garden almost to the water. He held exclusive and none-too-dignified parties, and installed one of his mistresses, Baronne de Vaughan. She presented him with two children. He married her three days before he died in 1909, but the Belgian authorities persuaded the Pope to annul the marriage immediately on the grounds of non-consummation. So Albert, his nephew, became king.

It was a successful restaurant from 1919 until the A13 motorway isolated it from the Paris traffic in the 1970s. In 1975, Janine Bourdrez and Jean Picard turned it into a delightful hotel, with modernized bedrooms, extra rooms in a fine old mansion with gardens across the country lane, tennis court, a swimming pool from which are views of the river, and a *vivier* to serve splendid lobsters.

King Leopold would have approved, although not perhaps of the gravel pits across the river visible in winter when the leaves are off the trees.

Seine barges queue to go through two locks just downstream, but the bedrooms are well soundproofed and little noise reaches up the hill. Bedrooms have modern but comfortable furniture and fittings. A new bar and summer dining room with splendid views has been built this year on the terrace, and a pleasant tea or aperitif room with really good reproductions of Impressionist paintings all round the walls.

The service is efficiently friendly, and I have found it difficult to make the effort to leave this delightful spot, especially as Mantes-la-Jolie upstream now has many tall modern buildings and factories and is not quite so 'jolie' any more. But I would not miss Giverny and the artist Claude Monet's house, garden and lily-pond (12km – see La Chaîne d'Or, Les Andelys, page 4).

LOCAL DRIVES

Paris 69km.
Mantes-la-Jolie
(9km) – incensed by insults
about his fatness and his love
of women made by Philippe I,
King of France, William the
Conqueror captured the town
and set it alight. A spark
frightened his horse which
threw him and he died six
days later in Rouen. The town
has the lovely fourteenth-
century chapel of Navarre in
its twelfth-century church.
Henry IV (Henry of Navarre)
switched for the second time
from Protestantism to
Catholicism here in 1593 after
the Catholic church had
cunningly offered him the
crown of France if he did so.
He is a national hero and the
French now maintain that he
said, 'If I do not accept, France
will cease to exist.' But history
records that he said more

cynically: 'Paris is worth a
mass.' Paris was delighted but
my ancestors weren't; they
obstinately remained
Protestant.

Versailles (52km) the
magnificent old royal palace
and gardens, not only one of
the most beautiful but one of
the most interesting buildings
in the world, needs at least a
day – and you should read a
book about it first.

Try the lobster
homard montgolfier

'Meals recommended by all the
culinary and tourist guides,'
says the guide *Châteaux Hotels
Indépendents*, and that includes *Michelin* (one star),
Gault Millau (high rating of 14
out of 20), and me!

Such fine ingredients su-
perbly cooked and presented
never come cheap, and young
Philippe Prevot does cook superbly, with a light touch.

His speciality is homard en
montgolfière (lobster from the
vivier in a white sauce with
truffles and mushrooms) but
lobster is even more outrageously dear in France than in
Britain and I have not tried it. I
have tried his huitres étuvées
au Champagne (oysters braised
in still Champagne) and they
are delicious.

I have also tried, as a special
treat, the middle-priced menu
royal and it was sheer delight –
salad of foie gras, then gratin of
scallops in a cream sauce, with
strips of vegetables (Julienne
de legumes). As a digestive
came a delicious water ice with
red wine. Then duck breasts in
lemon honey, the choice from
an outstanding platter of
several cheeses, and a very
special apple tart. It was
beautifully balanced and left
me happy but not bloated.

But down to earth. The
cheaper menu du marché is always good and lacks only wide
choice. Last time I had a plate
of excellent different pâtés. I
could have chosen creamed
mussels. I love duck confit
(preserved duck) and the one I
was given was canette (female
duckling) on a bed of green
cabbage and walnuts. Splen-

did. The alternative was escalope of salmon vigneronne – with grapes and wine. Then there was the cheeseboard and dessert of the day – this day, a chocolate fondant with two sauces of coffee and vanilla.

The wine list is reassuringly reasonable. Really good wines are much cheaper than in many lesser hotels and restaurants. The house red is a 1980 Bordeaux de la Closière, Muscadet and Sancerre (which is what I drink here with my first course) are both reasonable. There are pleasant Fleurie and Brouille reds from Beaujolais.

Last time I took with my duck a 1979 red of Gigondas. Gigondas wines from the Vaucluse (Rhône) can vary quite a lot,

and some are too acid for British palates. One of our greatest winebuyers, respected as a world expert, told me that Gigondas had a bouquet of manure! But an equal expert from France told me to go there just to taste the wines. I did; I ran into the wine fête at the neighbouring village of Sablet, stayed three days, saw a bull fight where, either from sympathy or economy, the bull was allowed to live, sat down with the whole village at tables in the square for 'un aioli' eating dried fish and tough beef smothered with garlic mayonnaise washed down with pints of local red wine from barrels parked strategically around the square. At midnight in the

square I was dancing with an elegant French girl from a local manor house to the music of Les Teddy Boys while Barbara danced close to a local version of Sacha Distel.

The Corniche Gigondas was a better wine. In fact it was very good. It came from the Meffres family Domaine des Bosquets, was strong in alcohol, warming, and reached the bottom of my heart as well as my stomach. Gigondas was often slipped into the better known Châteauneuf du Pape bottles in the bad old days. Now it is AC – appelation contrôlée – in its own right. Trust the Corniche to find such a good one.

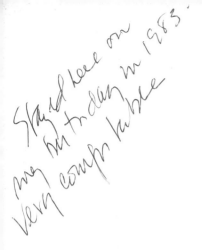

Château de Montreuil
62170 Montreuil sur Mer (off
N1, 38km from Boulogne).
Telephone: (21) 81.53.04.
Rooms F–H (breakfast
included);
menu weekdays B;
8-course degustation E;
card E–F.
Closed 3 January to 15
February.
Visa, Euro, Amex, Diners.

This is where I should like to celebrate my golden wedding – if I make it. Meanwhile it is ideal for a rejuvenating weekend. Easily reached from Boulogne or Calais by attractive routes, it is a pretty cream 'Edwardian' house in an English garden which might have strayed from Lyme Regis, tucked snugly under fearsome 700-year-old walls of medieval Montreuil, now topped by trees and a promenade with magnificent views across the Canche valley.

A hotel since the 1930s, it reached the stars – two from *Michelin* – then became very run down. It is now running up fast again under a charming and professional young couple. Patron-chef is Christian Germain, until two years ago chef de cuisine at the Waterside, Bray (owned by the Roux brothers). Christian is one of the best young chefs in France, even if *Gault Millau* failed to put him on their list. Lindsay, his English wife, is a charming professional hotelkeeper who has a flair for decoration. Without a fortune to

spend she has transformed the awful 1920s art-deco bedrooms into pleasant rooms with bright warmth, though leaving some of the funnier stucco decorations like monkeys and birds. Try to get a bedroom overlooking the delightful garden.

The Germans used this little château as an anti-invasion headquarters during the war. The Germains found a notice in the attic warning everyone entering to Heil Hitler! Napoleon's Marshal Ney had his 'invasion of England' headquarters here and Douglas Haig, British Army commander of the First World War, rates a bronze statue beside the big market square. His headquarters were at Château Beaurepaire, 6km away along N39.

Like Rye, Montreuil has not been 'sur mer' for centuries. Blessedly, the dreaded N1 bypasses it now. But in holiday season, visitors flock to its hilltop castle from which knights rode out to die at Crécy, its narrow streets flanked by lovely old buildings like the ancient Benedictine Abbey of St Saulve, and the flamboyant

Lovely!

Le Touquet, through the fishing port of Étaples. Touquet is one of the most underrated French resorts, with a massive sand beach, lovely forest, outstanding sports facilities such as riding, golf, swimming, sand-sailing, water-sailing and tennis, including indoors by natural light; smart shops including branches of Paris boutiques, superb fish shop and restaurant of Serge Pérard.

Hesdin (24km) is a charming little market town with a Renaissance church and town hall which was the sixteenth-century palace of Marie of Hungary, sister of Charles V, whose Spanish–Netherlands empire spread as far as here. Drive from Montreuil on little road north of the Canche river (not the ugly, lorry-ridden N39) through Beaurainville. Return to Montreuil through Hesdin forest to the north, on the D108 to Hucqueliers, then local roads west to Beutin and the D127.

The Authie river valley is attractive. Make for Maintenay, cross by an old water mill beside its millpond (now a pub, Vieux Moulin), then follow the south bank past Abbaye des Valloires, turning left for Hesdin later along the D928 at Labroye.

Boulogne's market is on Wednesday and Saturday mornings in Place Dalton; there is a fish market on the fish quay every weekday morning. Philippe Olivier runs the best cheese shop in France in rue Thiers, off Faidherbe.

fifteenth-century chapel with fine rich furnishings. Also its little shops, including one of the most amusing antique shops in France, medieval houses and the old Hôtel de France. When this was Hôtel du Roy, the eighteenth-century Yorkshire parson and writer Laurence Sterne, starting his *Sentimental Journey* distributed sous to a line of poor children as he stepped into his post chaise and announced: 'They do these things better in France.' He meant begging, not hotels.

From Boulogne or Calais, do not go to Montreuil by the N1. Take the N42 from Boulogne towards St Omer, turning soon on to the D341 through the attractive forest of Boulogne to the outskirts of Desvres, then right on little D127 through the valley of the river Course.

Food & Drink

Christian Germain must have been in a small dilemma when he left the Waterside in Bray for Montreuil. He had been working with the Roux brothers, who introduced the best of Nouvelle Cuisine's light touches to England, and moved to an area of France where traditional cooking still reigns, and butter and cream from the rich lush pastures are used as if European dairy mountains must be demolished by the weekend.

But the Roux team have never gone to those excesses which make both Frenchmen and foreign visitors feel that they are being forcibly slimmed and swin-

dled at the same time. And in North-West France it is no longer fashionable to ladle pints of cream into soup from bowls on the table.

Christian has already hit a very nice balance between Nouvelle and traditional cooking, all freshly cooked.

He uses Nouvelle's compulsory raspberry vinegar on a delightful oyster mousseline – made with puréed fish beaten with egg whites and thick cream and poached in a mould. He does believe in boiling everything right down to thicken sauces, avoiding flour where possible, but that is not new. Escoffier did it. And he is not afraid of butter and cream. His fresh-baked croissants are so rich that I can manage only one at breakfast.

I have seen him simmer an enormous pot of water containing beef bones, a few carrots and leeks, one bay leaf and a handful of salt for twelve hours, lidless, until it was down to a litre of thick stock, add six litres of red wine and boil down to one litre, add to that butter, shallots and a bottle of good Bordeaux red wine and make the best Bordelaise sauce I have ever tasted to put on steak.

I like his ramekins of chicken and goose liver or his onion soup with cider, as a starter – then his magnificent stuffed sea bass, and his chicken supreme rich in cream.

That sea bass: it is boned, with the head and tail left on, stuffed with chopped vegetable fennel, button mushrooms, thick cream and Pernod (the pastis aperitif). It is then reformed, wrapped in flaky pastry, glazed with egg yolk and baked. It is

served with a Hollandaise sauce lightened with whipped cream and a dash of Pernod – absolutely delicious.

Some of his sweets are not for slimmers: a superb marquise of melting chocolate-flavoured sponge rolled with Chantilly cream and fresh strawberries. And his apple pie: he lines the bottom of a pan completely with slices of hard butter, covers this entirely with sugar, then puts into this a layer of *eating* apples, cored, peeled and halved, heats very gently on top of the cooker until it caramelizes, then covers it with short pastry, bakes and serves with cream.

His fresh cheeseboard is filled from the maturing cellars in Boulogne of the master, Philippe Olivier, who buys not from factories but from farms all over France.

Christian had a fine wine cellar, until thieves stole the lot last year. He has replaced much, but some old wines were irreplaceable. Cheaper wines are well chosen. The house red is an AOC Bordeaux 1981, and the white a Bordeaux 1982 – both good value. I drink the Château Frontenac 1978 red or the good Verpoix Fleurie. I find most Fleurie much under-rated and way above most Beaujolais Villages. The Orfeuilles Muscadet is a good one, but the Sancerre Clos de Godons is my choice of whites. He used to have a gorgeous St Emilion Couvent des Jacobins 1974. I hope that the thieves choke on it. There is a fair choice of half bottles. When alone, I sometimes settle for half of white, then half of red.

Hostellerie les Champs

Hostellerie les Champs
Route d'Alençon-Rouen,
Gacé, Orne 61230.
Telephone: (33) 35.51.45.
Rooms B–D;
suites E;
menus A, B, C.
Closed 15 January to 15
February; Tuesdays lunch; all
Tuesdays out of season.
Euro, Diners.

Try the pâtisseries.
Patron-chef is helped by
24-year-old Etienne Robert -
one of the best young pastry
cooks in North France.

When Napoleon III was Emperor of France last century and aristocrats were having their last fling, a favourite hideout from Paris was the lush, park-like countryside of Orne in Normandy – land of rich pastures, hills, well kept forests, well groomed little garden towns such as the spa of Bagnoles, then very fashionable. Here they came to take the waters for previous excesses, gamble away fortunes in casinos, dance, make love and ride horses. At Gacé, on the outskirts, friends of the Grimaldis built a 'small', elegant and correct villa. The Grimaldis were Dukes of Gacé (a title which came down from Raoul, tutor to William the Conqueror) and rulers of Monaco. Prince Rainier stayed there as a young man.

Now we stay there as guests of the Tironneau family. The hotel is set among lawns and hundred-year-old trees, and although only a hundred yards from a main road it is very quiet. It has a heated swimming pool, tennis court and a prepared pitch for boules, the French national sport. It is tastefully furnished in a gently *fin de siècle* style with flowered wallpapers and much furniture of the Empire period, including chandeliers and china cabinets.

Our bedroom last time was the 'blue room' – a huge old bed of carved wood with a blue velvet headboard, sides and end, velvet-covered Empire chairs and a small settee, matching blue carpet, curtains and a huge wooden wardrobe. The modern bathroom was carpeted and had a reproduction of a Manet. I *do* like pictures in bathrooms and loos. Little touches included needle and cotton. It was good value.

On the second floor are four new suites decorated à la Laura Ashley.

Food & Drink

The Orne meadows, hills, woods and streams produce superb dairy products, game and river fish, especially outstanding trout, and the coast is near enough for daily deliveries of sea fish. Patron-chef

Haras du Pin (or Pin au Haras) – the French worship anything to do with thoroughbred horses, and this superb stud is set around the courtyard of a mansion designed by Mansart (royal architect) in 1716. The stud was founded by Jean Colbert, Louis XIV's finance minister. There are a hundred stallions here, including English and Irish thoroughbreds, French trotters, Norman cobs, Percherons and Anglo-Arabs. You can see them from between 9a.m. to noon and from 2 to 6p.m.

There is a racecourse and carriage-driving course. The Duke of Edinburgh has driven here.

Twelve km south of the stud is Château d'O, a gorgeous castle of Renaissance to eighteenth century reflected in its moat (open afternoons except Tuesday). Ten miles south of d'O begin shaded drives through the thick Ecouves forest, with picnic spots and little paths.

Bagnoles (69km) is delightfully, almost smugly, well tended, with casino and cure bath alongside a lake. The Great Spring water flows at 11,000 gallons an hour at 27°C/80°F, has few minerals but much radioactivity, and is used for circulation troubles, phlebitis, to prevent varicose veins and cure obesity. My doctor says I should live there . . . There are woodland walks to other pools, streams abound that are rich in trout.

Christian Tironneau uses these natural ingredients to produce mouth-watering meals without too many complications. Rather naturally, Normande sauce prevails – with lots of cream.

His cheapest menu is very pleasant, usually includes trout as a main-course choice, and among choice of starters is his soupe de poisson Dieppoise, one of his specialities. Don't be fooled by 'soupe'. It is poured over bread and is nearer to a stew than 'potage'.

The main difference between the second and third menus is that the second does not include entrée. It is good value, but Christian's entrées are very good.

Dishes on the card are well chosen, but many are on the menus, too, so unless one dish particularly takes your fancy, stick to the menus.

Mousse de poisson is among starters on all menus. Christian is rightly proud of it. Made with three different types of fish, it is delicately flavoured and floatingly light. Barbara says it is the best she has eaten.

For entrée, I would choose crêpe de saumon 'sauce Albert'. This, I agree, is not everyone's choice. The sauce was named after Prince Albert, who loved it, by Queen Victoria's chef, Francatelli, who invented it. It is made from young horseradish in thick cream with eggs and mustard. It is surprising how this brings out the flavour of salmon. Barbara, who does not like horseradish, adores the superb ficelle Normande – rolled pancake with a filling of ham, mushrooms and thick cream.

Christian's speciality for main course is lapereau à la Duchambais. I do not go over the top for wild rabbit, but this dish is an exception. Duchambais was a gourmet priest of Louis XIV's long reign. I know nothing more about him except that a method of cooking hare (lièvre) was named ater him – simmered with cream, shallots, wine-vinegar and pepper. Christian does it most successfully with rabbit.

He also cooks a beautiful caneton à la Bigarde for distrusters of rabbit, a Basque dish with the sauce made from the juice of roast duck mixed with bitter orange, which I find much tastier than sweeter orange sauce.

The Hostellerie's big cheese-

board is famous. Camembert is inevitably well represented, including the rare farmer's superbly creamy version, fruitier by far than the pasteurized commercial cheese.

The négresse en chemise, another speciality, is a lovely home-made chocolate ice covered in whipped cream, but I go for the fromage blanc Montmorency Cointreau – fresh soft natural cream cheese with cherries in Cointreau liqueur. Very tasty.

The wine list is very strong on Bordeaux reds, from a bargain La Naqueline to a delightful, deep coloured, deep flavoured Château Montrose St Estèphe – pricey, but nectar! Memories of the fine old vineyard by the river Gironde which still looks like an old château *cave*, not like a factory.

But first, the fish mousse deserves a more expensive white than I usually drink. Pouillysur-Loire, which, of course, has nothing to do with Pouilly Fuissé in Burgundy, produces whites from Sauvignon and Chasselas grapes, but only the best Sauvignon wines are called Pouilly-Fumé, and perhaps the best of these comes from Baron Ladoucette at Château Nozet just off N7. It is crisp, refreshing, not too flinty, though another wine made dearer by Parisian fashion.

With the rabbit or duck, you could have a Loire red, Bourgeuil, or a Bordeaux Château Rider Chenu Lafitte (not, of course, Lafite with one 't' as in Lafite-Rothschild, perhaps the greatest of clarets – there is a confusion of Lafittes in the Bordeaux area). If you could get by on half a bottle, try a very good St Emilion – Château St Valery Cheval Noir.

M. Tironneau recommends that you finish with an eighty-year-old Paradis Cognac. I don't like Cognac. I'll take his 1926 Calvados.

Don't skip the breakfast at Les Champs – two fresh croissants, fresh-baked bread, three sorts of home-made jam and a slab of Normandy farm butter – with fresh-squeezed orange juice and plenty of good coffee. Long live Old Normandy!

Hostellerie des Trois Mousquetaires
Château de la Redoute, 62120 Aire-sur-La-Lys, Pas-de-Calais (19km S of St Omer on N43; 10km NE of A26 motorway).
Telephone: (21) 39.01.11.
Rooms A–D;
menus A, B.
Closed mid-January to mid-February; Sunday evenings, Mondays.
Visa.

The château was built on the old Redoute fort, where d'Artagnan stayed.

Surely one of the greatest bargains in Europe. I was pointed to this nineteenth-century château, its lovely gardens and delightful traditional cooking many years ago by a Lille businessman when I was seeking refuge from the industrial zones. Now it is in nearly every guide book, has only eight bedrooms and pulls in eaters from as far as Lille (57km), Boulogne (60km), and Arras (56km), not to mention Britons heading to and from Paris on the motorway. So do book ahead.

With its pointed turrets, mullioned windows, and decorative timbers, it looks from outside like a cheerful fake. But its rooms inside are a delight, from the old salon where you can take an aperitif in clubland comfort, to the big cheerful dining room with a huge wood-fired rotisserie and immaculate cooking stoves and kitchen at one end – open plan, so that you can see what patron-chef Marcel Venet and his son Philippe are doing to your steak, guinea fowl or sauce.

Everything from armchairs to dining chairs is unashamedly comfortable. the bedrooms are a joy, most with pleasant views over the grounds, but there are two without their own bath and wc. They are pleasantly furnished in Louis XIII style. The gardens cover nearly eight acres, leading to the river, with old trees, fine lawns and a lake with swans and ducks.

The towers and belfries of Aire-sur-Lys make it look like a medieval painting. It is still an agricultural market town and has a vast square, Grand' Place, with eighteenth-century buildings, including a belfry and a fine town hall with a balcony for proclamations. Collegiate St Pierre, built in the fifteenth to seventeenth centuries, is one of the finest Flamboyant and Renaissance buildings in France. But the ornately sculpted and galleried Renaissance *bailliage* in Grand' Place is the local masterpiece.

I bet the old musketeer would have loved the wood-grilled steaks.

Food & Drink

The only guide which does not rate the Trois Mousquetaires is the *Gault Millau*. Surprise, surprise! The Venets grill over an open wood fire and produce some old local dishes with splendid old-fashioned sauces which are as far from Nouvelle Cuisine as you will get. Prices are incredibly low for such fine ingredients so well cooked, and there is plenty of choice on each course, even for the cheapest menus.

The cheapest weekday menu is unbelievably good value. You can start with a choice of salads, including fish, or ter-rines or tartlets, such as a fish quiche or leek tart (a great Flemish dish made with thick cream). Then you can have grilled steak, lamb chop or chicken, or choose from eleven dishes with lovely sauces, from steak au poivre to trout in white wine sauce. The local dish is potée (potful) with sausages and pork in a sort of soup-stew packed with lovely fresh local vegetables. You follow with a good choice of cheeses and a dessert from a long list which includes a favourite of mine – fresh pears poached in red wine of Burgundy, and Normandy tart (apples and almond pastry).

The most expensive menu, which costs the same as many of the cheapest menus of hotels in this selection, includes amongst its starters smoked salmon with scrambled eggs, frogs' legs, snails, and a plate of various home-made terrines. The main course includes contrefilet with a choice of four sauces, including a lovely Dijonnaise mustard sauce, served with cabbage gratin and excellent old-fashioned frîtes.

But, apart from grills, the specialities of the house are fresh fish brought that day from the coast, and I can recommend sole stuffed with smoked salmon, lotte (monkfish) in cider,

St Omer (19km) is the centre of waterways which lure painters. Fine merchants' houses of the sixteenth and seventeenth centuries. Notre-Dame in rue de l'Escugarie is a former cathedral of the thirteenth century, with a statue of Christ and tomb of St Omer, an eighteenth-century Benedictine monk.

Canals and waterways cover 300km, mostly past gardens to the forest of Clairmarais. The waters are rich in bream, tench, pike and eels, and surrounding market gardens grow some of the best cauliflower in Europe. The growers live in canalside cottages with paths over hump-backed bridges as their link with the world. Boat trips on the waterways, 'les Watergangs', lasting 1½ hours, leave from quite near the station.

Past St Omer (another 21km) on the N43 is Ardres, a pleasant little town which was the French front line under Francis I when the English held Calais, and Henry VIII's front-line headquarters were at Guines. This is a little old town 9km along D231 which seems to belong to France of the First World War, with little old bars and shops and squares of the past.

and brochette de St Jacques beurre Provençal (scallops grilled on a skewer, served with a sort of aïoli – a rich garlic mayonnaise). I have also had a delightful turbot with a sauce made from fragrant flowers of thyme.

The foie gras, made in the hotel by the son Philippe and his charming wife Caroline, is marinaded in Sauternes wine. It is delicious and not dear for foie gras. Philippe smokes the salmon, too.

Madame Venet, the smiling and welcoming wife of Marcel, not only looks after the restaurant superbly but invents some of the recipes.

A good sensible wine list with some tempting grander Bordeaux also has some good bourgeois and bourgeois supérieur wines, including a nice Médoc. But I would normally stick to the house Muscadet and a very drinkable 'Réserve Auberge' red at a price to match the bargain menus.

South from here, little white roads wind up and down hills in charming country, past Guines forest, with a hilltop memorial to the first men who crossed the Channel by balloon in 1785, Colonel Blanchard and the American Dr Jeffries. Just off the Guines–St Omer road is the site of the meeting of the Field of the Cloth of Gold, where Henry and Francis met in a display of rival pomp to discuss an alliance. Henry left after Francis had thrown him at wrestling, and made an alliance with the rival Charles V. Another summit which went wrong.

Follow the pretty little white roads through hamlets, past the forest of Tournehem, to St Omer.

Manoir de Moëllien

**Manoir de Moëllien
Plonévez-Porzay, 29127
Plomodiern, Finistère,
Brittany (Manoir is marked
on *Michelin* yellow map 58;
on D107 drive 2km past
Plonévez-Porzay, take C10
lane on left. From Locronan
take C10 from opposite Hotel
Hermitage 3km; 20km from
Quimper, 9km Douarnenez).
Telephone: (98) 92.50.40.
Rooms E;
menus B, C, D;
half-board E;
Closed part November,
December; open Christmas
and New Year; closed
January.
Visa, Euro, Diners.**

A stunningly beautiful silver-grey, stone Breton manor of 1642, it was taken over as a virtual ruin by Marie Anne Le Corré's grandmother. In the last few years Mme Le Corré and her husband have totally restored it, using original stone, and it is a masterpiece. There is a big square tower, a superb old doorway, and on the stonework the coat of arms of the Moëllien family who built it. Their motto in Bretton '*Sell Pobl*' means 'Be concerned about People'. Mme Le Corré keeps to this motto. A stay here is not just good value – it is a bargain.

The rooms are magnificent. The big dining room is impressive and inviting. Massive beams across the ceiling top stone walls, a great stone fireplace and a floor in coloured tiles. Any overpowering effect the stone might have is softened by big windows, pretty striped curtains, two long paintings of medieval ladies, painted on silk by artists from the craft village of Locronan, and old Breton furniture, including a superb sideboard and exquisite carved wardrobe.

The bedrooms are in attractive old stone stables. They are are charming rooms, all with French windows leading on to a path and lawns with views over the countryside. The grounds are laid out in lawns, paths and flowering shrubs, with masses of hydrangeas. The sea and fine sand beaches lie 3km away.

A Relais du Silence.

LOCAL DRIVES

Locronan (3km S on C10): like an English village built in granite. A beautiful town which made a lot of money for centuries weaving sailcloth for the French navy. Rich merchants built fine Renaissance houses around a wide cobbled square with the ancient town well in the middle. It faces a sixteenth-century flamboyant Gothic church dedicated to St Ronan, the Irishman who converted this part of Brittany. He is buried in the church, and for centuries pilgrims came to his grave. Locronan today is a ville d'art, with artisans working in glass and wood and weaving in wool, linen and silk. A museum of contemporary art shows Breton scenes, furniture and costumes.

Douarnenez (9km on D107): on the Pouldavid estuary it is an historic fishing port, once with sardine boats, now mackerel, some tunny, but mostly crayfish and langoustines. Streets of the old quarter zig-zag down to the sea and the quays are still lively and colourful. There is superb scenery around the bay which encloses the perhaps-legendary town of Ys, submerged by the sea. An isle in the estuary, St Tristan, was the headquarters of the sixteenth-century brigand La Fontenelle-Ligeur who terrorized Brittany. Fish is still auctioned on Rosemeur harbour. Boat and sea-fishing trips for tourists leave here in high summer. Over the big steel river bridge is Tréboul, sailing centre and school, with narrow streets round a little port.

Pointe du Raz (32km): take D7 from Tréboul, interesting and spectacular route; a road right leads to Cap Sizun, seabird reserve in a wild setting. Trépassés Baie (Bay of the Dead) was where Druids were taken across for burial on Sein Island. Men of Sein are fishermen and regarded even digging fields as women's work until recently. Once they lived by luring ships on rocks and wrecking them – like Isles of Scilly. In June 1940 the entire male population, even thirteen-year-olds, sailed to England to join the Free French. The tidal race here is frightening. A great Atlantic swell rolls magnificently into the bay. Raz Point is a tourist spot – cafés, souvenir shops, crêperies.
Quimper (19km SE): see Manoir du Stang, La Forêt-Fouesnant page 22.

Food & Drink

We have had here some of the best value meals in two or three years. Bruno Garet, well known in Brittany, is now chef, and the card is altogether more ambitious without great price increases. There is a simple cheap menu, which Barbara had for lunch, of rillettes of mackerel in anis, or melon dowsed in Pineau de Charentes (brandy and young wine mixed) for starters, fricassé of duck with grapefruit, which she chose, or filet d'Anon au beurre as main course. Anon, it seems, is a Breton name for a haddock, which Barbara says is an anonymous fish until

smoked. Then you can have sorbet or a choice of the good house pâtisserie.
But for dinner it must be the card or the dearest menu, which is still not very dear.
First you can have Breton oysters, raw salmon marinaded in fresh lime juice and dill (a rather aniseedy herb used by our ancestors for fish before lemons were flown in) or crème d'étrilles (a little Breton crab in cream sauce). Next course was St Jacques à la nage – scallops poached in white wine, shallots, herbs and cream – a dish I love, or the chef's speciality, which you just have to try. It is feuilleté de turbot au beurre de poireaux.
The main course was duck

breast in apricot or entrecôte steak in a Roquefort sauce. Choice of cheeses is good because they are all from farms, not factory. Desserts include a choice of three sorbets – Dijonnaise (cassis sorbet with crème de cassis), Normande (apple sorbet with Calvados, a great digestive) and Colonel (lemon sorbet with vodka).
It is a very good meal, but a little disappointing in the meat course if, like me, you have tired of duck breasts with fruit. Next time I shall back the card, with a dozen oysters to start, the marinaded salmon as the next course, and the turbot as main course. You cannot get fish much fresher than here, 9km from where it is landed.

20 *Pas de Calais/Normandy/Brittany*

There is a good wine list from many parts of France, including a whole card of red Bordeaux, a few great wines, and many good ones at most reasonable prices for a Château Hôtel Indépendant. There is a wide choice of white wines, which is proper in fish country. Some French hotels do not take white wine seriously enough. They take the attitude of my youth: 'A bottle of white wine is what two gentlemen drink while they are deciding which red to choose.' There are also plenty of half-bottles.

Among the whites you do not meet so often outside their regions is a Beaujolais blanc, which I find dull; a nice cheap Quincy, a fairly rare crisp Sauvignon wine from near Sancerre; a white from the Chapoutier property at St Joseph, opposite Hermitage on the Rhône and producing nearly all red wine, and another Chapoutier white from Hermitage itself which is dry and full and one of the two best produced there. It is called Chante Alouette, is the dearest white on the list, and worth every franc. Shellfish, fish and meat or duck, you could drink it through all three courses. It is more powerful than white Burgundy.

Another interesting white is a Châteauneuf du Pape from the biggest estate there – Domaine de Mont Redon. I have not tried it, but their reds are strong, robust wines.

If you like rosé with your fish, there is a still 'pink' Champagne (Coteau Champenois) which would be interesting.

MANOIR DU STANG

**Manoir du Stang
29133 La Forêt-Fouesnant,
Sud-Finistère, Brittany
(private drive off D783, 13km
SE Quimper, 8km NW
Concarneau).
Telephone: (96) 56.97.37.
Rooms E–H (much size
variation); some apartments
for 3; you are expected to have
one meal in the hotel each
day;
menus B (lunch), D;
half-board (2 sharing) G, H.
Closed mid-September to mid-
May except for groups and
conferences.**

The sixteenth-century stone manor house is beautiful. The hundred-acre gardens and park are outstandingly beautiful. It has belonged to the same family for two centuries and was made into a hotel fifty years ago – one of the first big old châteaux to be converted. It was my first 'castle', too, when I stayed there in the 1950s, and I was captivated. It is even better now, having been much renovated in 1958 from wartime decay.

It is superbly furnished with antiques and wood panelling of its own period. But it is the grounds which make me so loath to leave: beautiful flowered terraces laid out in the formal French style; rose gardens; lawns and copses with laid-out paths; big lakes where you can fish; paths through woods and beside crops; a tennis court; and a kitchen garden which supplies the hotel. The grounds run almost to the sea.

It is a peaceful place to hide away with someone you love. The service is discreet and charming, the guests I have met *très gentils*. It is a perfect base for seeing an attractive and interesting part of Brittany. Within 2km radius are a beach, golf, horse riding and the new Port de Plaisance of La Forêt-Fouesnant, with swimming pool, sailing school, boats for sea-fishing, and boat trips round to Bénodet and up the river Odet or to the Glénan Isles; on one isle is a famous sailing school, on another a skin-diving school, and some are bird sanctuaries uninhabited by humans. Terns abound.

Fouesnant, 3km W, is a village among cherry and apple orchards and makes the best cider in Brittany. It is known for the costumes and coiffes (headdresses) worn by the girls on such occasions as the Pardon of Sainte Anne, which is based on a chapel in a pretty setting 3km N. The Pardon is on 26 July and the following Sunday. These Breton pardons are festivals with hymn singing, processions, banners, statues of saints, and church services for the forgiving of sins, followed by dancing,

Concarneau (8km) is the third largest fishing port in France, with a harbour to take fleets of trawlers and tunny boats, and a walled town dating from before the days of William the Conqueror. Despite restaurants and souvenir shops within the Ville Close, it looks much as it did 300 years ago when the 'impregnable fortress' of the fourteenth-century was made even more impregnable by the great military architect Vauban for Louis XIV. The English held it for thirty years and it took the Breton hero du Guescelin to get them out. Early most mornings you can see the fishing boats taking aboard their traditional blue nets before sailing. One of France's most colourful festivals is Concarneau's Fêtes des Filets Bleus (Feast of the Blue Nets) on the second from last weekend in August. Pont Aven (14km on) is a nice resort where the river Aven runs into an estuary. You may recognize scenes painted by Gauguin, including the sixteenth-century wooden Christ in Kermalo chapel. He started a school here for lesser artists in the 1890s, preaching, 'Paint what you see, not what is there.' He fell out with the fishermen, had a punch-up and broke a leg. There are none of his paintings in the local museum.

Beg Meil (9km from the Manoir) – a little port with lobster boats and huge sand beach with pine tree shade was my old favourite; now crowded in high season with cars parked everywhere. Benodet (12km) is a lively beach resort, attractive but it has many camp sites, so crowded.

Quimper (13km) – a delightful chaotic market town with narrow streets, and a huge Gothic cathedral with lacey spires, the market near it spilling out to block nearby streets, especially on Saturday; despite parking problems it is well worth visiting. The rivers Odet and Steir meet here.

sports, feasting, drinking and possibly committing a few new sins before morning.

Brittany has 7847 saints, mostly Celtic monks who led the fifth-century migration from Britain and whose special powers will help to fight any ill, tragedy or misfortune in humans or animals. My favourite is St Sansom, a North Welshman from a Glamorgan monastery, who defeated a dragon by singing psalms to it, which made it roll itself into a ball and start eating its tail. Then he told it to drop dead and it did. Much the same happens to English rugby teams when Welsh fans sing 'Land of My Fathers'.

Food & Drink

Guy Hubert likes his guests to stay at least three days if possible to enjoy this lovely house and gardens, which would be no hardship. Although every care is taken with food and cooking, he says that cuisine is not the most important item here.

I think that he is being modest. The cooking of Roland Flao may not be in the three-star *Michelin* class but it is very good, especially the fish. White fish and shellfish are excellent in this part of Brittany and, sensibly he cooks them traditionally with good sauces rather than trying to invent a clever dish.

The sole soufflée au homard (lobster), which has to be ordered ahead, has been described as 'on the way to perfection' and the soupe de poisson was the favourite of Anne Con-

way, our photographer, who lives in France. Barbara settled for a starter of local huîtres creuses (oysters) from the bay down the road. Being one of the world's great consumers and very fond indeed of shellfish, I paid a little more on the menu for a plateau de fruits de mer. There is a big platter on the card which could be taken as a whole meal. In fact, you might not manage much after it except sorbet or fruit.

The fish course on the menu when we were there was a choice of poached turbot with beurre blanc (shallots cooked in butter and whisked with white wine), which was delicious, and brochette of scallops (coquilles St Jacques), a house speciality. The main course was grilled entrecôte steak 'maître d'hôtel' (with parsley butter), served with potatoes, carrots and tomatoes. A perfectly good steak, and nice vegetables, but rather dull. Next time I shall take the card and stick to fish. There was salad, too. The cheeseboard was a little thin but in good condition – Camembert, St Paulin, and a goat's cheese.

The menu sweet course was sorbet or ice cream, a pity because there were some splendid pâtisserie and other desserts on the card.

Not a bad meal for the price. But next time I shall go for the card – the local oysters or local palourdes (clams) with butter and parsley and grilled, followed by that sole soufflée au homard or if lobsters are not too pricey in the market place, homard à l'Armoricaine, that gorgeous piquant sauce of white wine, brandy, garlic,

shallots and tomatoes which brings out all the flavour of lobster.

The waitresses wear traditional Breton costumes.

Wines are reasonably priced for these days in a hotel of this standard and the list well chosen. The 1980 Chablis was very good. The 1976 Grand Corbin St Emilion red is a bargain. These two would suit the menu. But if on my own or with someone with my slightly offbeat taste in what to drink with lobster, I would have the Muscadet sur lie with the oysters and the Bouchard Beaune de Château (a splendidly blended wine with high quality wines in it) with the lobster or the sole soufflée with lobster. Burgundy and lobster have never upset me yet, and Beaune goes nicely with Armoricaine sauce. It has enough flavour to break through.

Old French hospitality in lovely surroundings

Moulin du Vey
Le Vey, 14570 Clécy (35km S of Caen, on D133A from Clécy, just over river Orne).
Telephone: (31) 69.71.08.
Rooms D, E; apartments for 4 F; if full in season, more rooms at annexe Relais de Surosne (3km);
menus B, C, E;
half-board F.
Closed Fridays in winter.

I don't normally recommend mixing wine and water but they make a perfect soporific at Moulin du Vey. A bottle of La Grappe des Papes from Châteauneuf in the dining room of this converted water-mill, the background music of the Orne river flowing fast over low rapids, and I can sleep untroubled.

It is a magical spot, with creeper and roses almost hiding the old mill, and a little balustraded boardwalk to the arm of the river which used to drive the mill. You can sit under umbrellas on lawns watching the river tumble down those rapids to a mid-stream island, swallows diving over you.

Across the river, beside a café, canoeists set out to shoot the rapids then paddle on down river round a wide bend.

Rooms are prettily furnished in period or country style. My bedroom last year had two ornate but pretty big double beds and curvy empire period furniture. The dining room opens on to the lawns beside the river.

It is a delightful place for a weekend or a week. There are riverside and woodland walks, good fishing, boating, canoeing, swimming in the river, riding nearby. Or you can laze and watch others using the river.

Food & Drink

Chef Michel Choplin is the son-in-law of the sympathetic owner Denise Leduc. He uses the great raw materials of the Suisse Normande to offer traditional local dishes with his own touches of invention. He cooks fish, especially fresh river fish, superbly – and the trout and sandre swim past the lawn.

The cheapest menu disappointed some of my friends but not me nor the *Gault Millau*, which recommends it. Last time I had it, the choice of starters was gorgeous creamed mussels or a tasty terrine des trois poissons, which can be extremely bland if poorly prepared. Then came trout stuffed with pike or tripes mode de Caen; cheese, and dessert (this

LOCAL DRIVES

The Orne is a lovely river, winding through park-like pastures, woods and gentle hills. Britons are just discovering it in a small way, particularly Bagnoles (46km from Clécy), the beautifully-groomed spa with lake, woods, many restaurants and, today, too many people. Its waters are taken to improve circulation. (I once sent some to one of my editors, but he did not see the joke.) At Pont d'Ouilly (12km) you can follow the Orne on a lovely route to Putanges- Pont-Écrepin (an old town with fine main square, river bridge and photogenic setting) or take the valleys of the Noireau and Vère to Flers (a sixteenth-century moated castle – 24km), passing beneath some tall escarpments and round some blind turns. Narrow roads from Putanges pass through the Gorges de St Aubert to some superb views. Most spectacular is Roche d'Oëtre, a glorious spot overlooking wriggling gorges of the Rouvre river cutting its way to the Orne.

Caen (37km) is modern, reconstructed after war damage. It is pleasant, industrial, a good shopping centre. Part of St Etienne church was built by William the Conqueror and Lanfranc, whom he made Archbishop of Canterbury. William was buried here, but the tomb was plundered later. Beyond Caen are the D-Day landing beaches and the family seaside resorts of Calvados.

time strawberries and cream).

From the good starters on the card I can recommend St Jacques feuilleté Nantais, scallops with white wine sauce, mushrooms and mussels, and salade de deux poissons fumés. He has a fine salmon pâté, too. On the main course his simpler dishes of high quality ingredients are excellent – braised duck, noix de veau (topside of veal), shoulder of lamb. If you like sweetbreads (ris de veau) he cooks them well in Vouvray wine. A lovely dessert is lemon mousse with orange syrup.

The masterpiece of the house is the gastronomic fish menu – several courses from salmon pâté and mousseline de brochet (pike mousse) building up to a climax with lobster. Sitting opposite me one night was one of those tall, slim, perfectly-dressed Frenchmen with iron grey hair, and an elegant, superbly groomed, handsome lady of about forty. I watched them work their way correctly

and almost daintily through this fish meal. With it they drank just two bottles of champagne – Veuve Clicquot, Carte d'Or, 1976. I was alone – and jealous.

At the other end of the scale, you could drink the local sparkler – cidre bouché.

This is Muscadet country, and the Muscadet Fief de la Cormeraye is fruity and refreshing – one of the best. But I tried the fairly-rare white wine of the Upper Loire, Quincy, a nice crisp wine made from Sauvignon grapes.

The Châteauneuf du Pape 'La Grappe des Papes' is a classic wine and not dear, but there are some very drinkable cheaper red wines on the list – a Côtes du Rhône, a Château Fontenac Bordeaux and a Bordeaux La Closière. There are also Bordeaux and Burgundy of many châteaux right up to a 1952 Mission Haut Brion and an Hospice de Beaune 1964. For that sort of wine it is no good being alone – and jealous!

Perfect – a bottle of wine alongside the fast-flowing Orne river here.

LE REPAIRE DE KERROC'H

**Le Repaire de Kerroc'h
22 quai Morand, 22500
Paimpol, Côtes-du-Nord,
North Brittany (120km from
St Malo; 44km NW of St
Brieuc; 28km N of Guingamp).
Telephone: (96) 20.50.13.
Rooms F; apartment G;
menus A, C, D;
half-board F.
Closed part of January.
Visa, Euro, Amex, Diners.**

The old pirate Pierre Corouge Kersaux, who made a good thing out of the French Revolution, built this house on Paimpol harbour front in 1793 to keep an eye on the boats – his own and other people's. Now all the bedrooms overlook the harbour, but you see brightly-coloured yachts rather than corsairs or fishing boats, though one or two might be involved in a bit of smuggling.

To a yachtsman or fisherman, Le Repaire is a little heaven. To anyone addicted to beautiful fresh fish, harbour scenes, and cosy, comfortable and intimate bedrooms it is a superb place to stay. Robert and Lyliane Abraham have already made improvements in two years, like double glazing the bedroom windows so that you can enjoy the harbour without being awakened early by its noise.

Another noise-killer is the hessian wall covering in the bedrooms. The rooms are all different, small, furnished with good taste, and with excellent bathrooms. Ours had deep blue walls and tiles with blue roses, and looked warmly

charming. The bedrooms have mini-bar, radio and telephone. We stole the only room with a balcony – a fine spot for watching people messing about in boats.

I *should* call Pierre Corouge Kersaux a corsair, not a pirate, for he was a pirate licensed by the French King. That must have been a great consolation to the crews of the merchantmen he killed. Walking the Plank by Royal Charter.

Kersaux joined the French Revolutionaries and became the most important man in the region, starting the Tribunal de Commerce Maritime de Paimpol and making himself president from 1790 to 1815, with power over all sea trade and ships' armaments. A nice number until Napoleon was defeated. His house (the hotel) is a national historic monument.

Food & Drink

The dining room overlooks the harbour and the new chef-patron Robert Abraham knows what is expected of him – the best, fresh fish, well prepared and cooked immaculately. Not many guests stray far from fish, although he has two meat dishes, and one, dos d'agneau farci aux champignons (saddle of lamb stuffed with mushrooms), has been much praised. Barbara thinks that he is one of the best fish chefs in France.

While you are choosing your meal he offers an Amuse-gueule – an appetizer. It may be rillettes of mackerel, small tomatoes in a cream sauce, mushrooms in garlic or rillettes of another fish or meat.

There is a cheap menu marin on which many people lunch. First you have six local oysters and local clams. Then la dariole de christes-marines aux moules. Dariole is a small bucket-shaped pastry, christes-marines are samphires, which are cliff plants with saline fleshy leaves (I did not know that, either) and moules are, of course, mussels (I knew that!). Then blanquette de lieu (pollack), and then came soft cream cheese with herbs or the special dessert of the house.

We tried an excellent middle-priced menu. With all those oyster beds in the bay, we simply had to choose poached oysters and winkles (bigorneaux) in a butter and cream sauce, despite other temptations. The dish won Robert the Grand Prix d'Honneur at the Concours Culinaire at Vannes in 1982. Then we chose dés de lotte relevés au beurre de saumon fumé. Dés means thimbles and this was small rounds of monkfish (an ugly looking but nicely flavoured fish called lotte which the

Arcouest Point (6km N by D789) for the boat to isle of Bréhat; at the little village of Ploubazlanec on D789 is a cemetery with a sad wall carrying names of all local men lost at sea over the centuries. Pointe d'Arcouest has splendid views over Paimpol Bay on its way down to the creek. It was recommended to me in the early 1950s as the ultimate place to get away from tourists in Brittany. Then it was discovered by artists, writers and academics who made an annual summer invasion. Now its hotel has a swimming pool. But much of the year it is sleepy. There is a tiny lobster port. Take a boat to Bréhat, an island refuge from motor cars, which are banned. It has beaches of shingle and paths between scrub and stone-walled fields which join little low houses pointing inwards against the north and west winds. But winters are mild, and mimosa, oleander, myrtle and figs grow in the open. The island's fishermen were fishing Newfoundland banks before Columbus 'discovered' America and a local sea-captain Coatanlen is said to have told Columbus about the New World and the course used by fishermen eight years before he sailed. Loquivy-de-la-Mer (5km N of Paimpol by D786, then D15) – a tiny lobster fishing port in a creek; 'quaint'.

French love). They were placed round the edge of a plate with a few slices of cour-gette and a courgette gâteau in the middle, served with a sauce of smoked salmon butter. It was delicious – some of the best lotte we have had.

The cheeses are superbly chosen. They were in perfect condition. I should like to lunch on a little of each. They included Brillat (a mild creamy Normandy cheese, surprisingly only first produced in the 1930s yet now copied all over France); Fourme d'Ambert (from the Auvergne and blue veined but *not* Bleu d'Auvergne which is sharp in smell and flavour and made in a big, flat disc while this is tall and cylindrical, has a fruity flavour and is made by small farms around Montbrison); Chèvre de Selles-sur-Cher (goat's cheese from Touraine) and Charolais (dry goat's milk cheese from Burgundy); Abbaye d'Entrammes (a fruity, bendy cheese made by the monks at their farm, originally the site of the monastery of Port du Salut; the cheese was called Port-Salut until that name was sold to a commercial producer); Chevrotin des Aravis (firm mild goat's cheese from Massif des Aravis in the Savoy, left to mature for over a year).

The Palette des desserts du Repaire is a large plate of six different desserts – sorbet in a tulip biscuit, slice of apricot tart, coffee mousse, lemon mousse on mint leaves with strawberry sauce, chocolate truffle and lemon-curd tart.

A very good value menu. For a few pounds more you could have a huge plateau of fruits de mer with half a lobster – a meal in itself.

Breakfast comes on a trolley – fresh orange juice, lots of coffee, hot croissant and toast in a bag to keep it hot, salt and unsalted butter, honey, two jams and a plate of cherries.

Most of the red wines have been well picked to accompany fish. You could choose the very reasonably priced co-operative Marquis de Saint Estèphe 1979, a good year producing fruity wines, not too dry or thin as in some bad years. Then there is a fine St Emilion Clos Trimoulet 1980, one I like particularly. It is a *grand cru* (great growth) which in St Emilion ranks oddly below *premier cru*, but it means the wine is usually first class, so to speak, if not magnificent. For a lighter, sharper wine to take with fish, try the Loire Saumur Champigny red Domaine des Roches Neuves of Denis Duveau. Good value here.

For your shellfish, or if you stick to the 'white with fish' rule, the choice is small but good. There is a very good Sancerre, Le Chêne Marchand from Pichard-Crochet. Experts say this wine has deteriorated in recent years but I have not noticed. One of my favourite Muscadets is there – Château de la Bretesche. But if you are celebrating, try a magnum of the best Pouilly Fumé now produced – Baron Patrick Ladoucette's wine from his Château du Nozet called Baron de L. Don't forget to drink to the Baron, who has personally put fire back in Fumé.

Le Saint Pierre

Le Saint Pierre
place du Bateau, La Bouille,
76530 La Couronne, Seine-
Maritime (on S bank of the
Seine 20km W of Rouen; 3km
from motorway A13 Rouen-
Caen; on D93 from junction of
N138 and N180).
Telephone: (35) 23.80.10.
Rooms D, E;
menus B, D, E.
Closed 30 October to 16
November, part February;
Tuesday evenings,
Wednesdays in winter.
Visa.

This hotel is right on the bank of the Seine (*les pieds dans l'eau*), separated from the water by an old towpath, now a terrace with tables for drinking on bright days. I was woken one morning around seven by metallic bumping noises coming through the open window and looked up to see the superstructure of a barge a few feet from my bed. Two enormous great modern Seine barges, very clean and neat, had tied up alongside the tiny pier so that a bargee could climb perilously round the pier gate and cross the road to buy a paper and a dozen baguettes – the traditional long French loaves.

Quite frankly, I have chosen this riverside hotel not for its comfort, décor or furnishings but for its position by the river, its usefulness as a bolthole from Rouen (a lovely old city overpowered now by its industries, traffic, concrete and flyovers), the near-quaintness of the riverside village of La Bouille, the enthusiastic welcome of Bernard Huet and his wife, and the cooking of young Patrice Kukurudz.

There is nothing wrong with the bedrooms. They are comfortable and nice with efficient and pleasant bathrooms. I just find far-eastern flavour a bit contrived and out of place on the Seine, especially with a barge looking through the window. Never mind. I am very fond of Le Saint Pierre, and so are a lot of other Britons. So book ahead, especially on weekends in summer when the people of Rouen come out here to eat. The bar is open to the public, which is interesting to me. I like to sit and watch other people.

La Bouille is little more than a road of timbered old Norman houses and shops, restaurants and hotels along the riverside road. The painter Monet loved it, and, apart from cars, would notice few changes. The car ferry still runs across the river to the Roumare forest. There were dozens of those down the Seine until the building of the Tancarville and Brotonne bridges put most of them out of business. Boats also go to Rouen on trips.

Rouen: take D67, then right on D64 to the Château de Robert-le-Diable (Robert the Devil) now in ruins and a pleasure garden; Robert the Devil was a mythical character based on Robert the Magnificent, father of William the Conqueror by a tanner's daughter. This Robert probably built the castle. It was blown up by the French in the fifteenth century to stop the English using it. There are fine river views, especially from the great tower. Also a Viking museum (closed Tuesdays), and at the meeting of D64 and D67 the Qui Vive monument with remarkable views of the curving Seine and Roumare forest. Reach Rouen through Rouvray Forest, a heath with clumps of pines. Rouen was completely redesigned after terrible war damage and is a modern city built for industry. But the old part, restored, is a joy. Start as everyone does at the Place du Vieux Marché, once the covered market, now an ultra-modern architectural complex, partly surrounded by pretty half-timbered houses of the seventeenth to eighteenth centuries. Eight, new, small covered markets are in the square, but it is dominated by the 65 foot (20 metre) Cross of the Rehabilitation on the spot where Joan of Arc was burned on 30 May 1431, and the very modern Church of St Joan, like a ship's hull inside, designed to take the wonderful sixteenth-century glass originally in St Vincent church destroyed in 1944. This remarkable tapestry of glass telling the story of Christ in superb colour covers 10,764 square feet (1000 square metres). Joan's statue leans against the church. I shall not try to guide you round Rouen in a few lines. You need a book about the city. The information centre is opposite the cathedral, round the corner from rue du Gros-Horloge which joins the cathedral to Vieux Marché and which has the famous clock that straddles the road.

Patrice Kukurudz joins Christian Germain of the Château de Montreuil as my favourite young chef in France. His *Michelin* star is well-earned and if *Gault Millau* is lukewarm about him, I suspect that is because he does not follow the Nouvelle fashion slavishly, though he does cook duck in cider vinegar – I prefer the old-fashioned Norman cider.

There are five menus, none very cheap, but all good value because of their high standards. The fish is so good here that the temptation is to pick from the card and have an all-fish meal.

Last time I chose the middle-priced menu. Starters were marbré de ris de veau (veal sweetbreads in hazelnut whipped cream sauce) or terrine of sole, which I chose. It was made with chervil and served with a cream parsley sauce.

The choice on the fish course was difficult – truite de mer (my favourite salmon trout) with a confit of leeks or mousseline d'écrevisses, which I chose. This is a superb way of serving crayfish – beaten with egg-whites and cream and poached. It was really light and very tasty.

I was ready for my sorbet au Calvados, the modern substitute for the good old 'trou Normand' – a good slug of neat Calvados taken in the middle of a big meal to help the digestion by making a hole (trou). Some say that this is a false theory. I find it true, so to speak!

There was a handsome-looking filet de boeuf en croûte, sauce Périgourdine (fillet steak in pastry with a truffled sauce), but you cannot get as near to Rouen as this and pass up a civet de caneton Rouennaise, even if Rouen duck comes not from Rouen these days but from around Yvetot or Duclair. It is still cooked the same way – stuffed with liver and the sauce thickened with its own blood.

A salad came next, then a lovely choice of Normandy cheeses, including Livarot (like a stronger, smellier Camembert with a red crust and quite delightful), a genuine Pont l'Evêque, so often badly imitated, and a good Port Salut. Desserts included a Calvados soufflé. I loved it.

The service is excellent, presided over by the charming Madame Huet. Bernard Huet serves the wines. He has a formidable cellar. There are 27 different Champagnes, 56 different clarets, 36 red Burgundies, 16 white Burgundies, a few Rhône wines, 4 Beaujolais, and the odd white Bordeaux, Loire, Alsace and Jura. They are all very good handpicked wines from some of the best producers and are not cheap. Only a handful are under 100F.

There is a fair choice of half-bottles for loners who are not too thirsty.

Of the less costly wines, the Sancerre Les Romains white comes from one of the very best producers, Marcel Gitton and I can recommend it not only for its fine fruity flavour but for the way it lingers on the tongue. At double the price, there is what I think to be the best Pouilly Fumé – Baron de L. produced by the go-ahead Baron Patrick Ladoucette, who uses the most modern methods of viniculture to control acidity. This is a white worth trying with Patrice's splendid fish.

Of the cheaper reds, I would go for Jaboulet's 1980 Grand Pompée from St Joseph, opposite Hermitage. I was most impressed by it, though I am told that the 1979 was even better. For a lightish luncheon red wine at a lower price, try the Beaujolais from Chiroubles, which comes from Beaujolais' highest hill vineyards. It is very easy to drink and would go just as well with salmon or duck as a light claret.

Of the dearer wines, they are all so good and well chosen that it is a question of pocket and personal taste. I can highly recommend the 1978 La Lagune Médoc, a third growth vineyard owned by Ayala Champagne company and which should be rated higher. This 1978 was outstanding – a lovely perfume, fine flavour, strong and really satisfying. I know because I was lucky enough to buy several cases of it at a bargain price. Another under-estimated claret here is the Margaux Château Brane Cantenac, a large property with just the right gravelly soil, and carefully produced. Others well worth their price are the Saint Julien second-growth Leoville Barton and the Château Figeac first-growth St Emilion, a rich, velvety wine, different from other St Emilions. The two very best St Emilions are there at a price – Ausone and Cheval Blanc.

Chosen mainly for its superb position by the river.

ti al lannec

ti al lannec
allée de Mézo-guen, 22560 Trébeurden, Côtes-du-Nord, North Brittany (on D786, the road round North Brittany coast from near St Malo 160km; 74km from Roscoff). Telephone: (96) 23.57.26 Rooms E; menus B, C, D; half-board E. Closed mid-November to mid-March; restaurant closed Monday lunch. Visa.

For many years this has been one of my very favourite seaside hotels anywhere, because of its position, its tasteful furnishings, the charm of its building, its excellent cooking of fresh local food, and above all for its atmosphere and the welcome from Gérard and Danielle Jouanny.

A granite manor house, hidden from the road by its trees, drive and lawns, it stands high above the bay and yacht harbour with great views from its terrace to the little islands, and in good weather to the north coast of Finistère. The grounds drop sharply below the terrace through trees and shrubs with a private path down to the beaches. You get the same superb views from the sun lounge-style dining room. The hotel is very pleasantly furnished, mostly with old pieces. The cosy lounge has a pleasant tapestry, there is a real bar outside the dining room. All bedrooms are different and are tastefully decorated. Most have big windows and all have bathrooms. Some have balconies looking to sea and two have small sitting rooms.

Although this is a Relais du Silence, the family are very helpful in looking after children and provide a children's meal; but I don't think Trébeurden is the best place for toddlers because of its steep hills – unless you want to drive every time you go to the beach. It's a pleasant little old-style resort, excellent for children about seven and over. It has several crescents of fine sand divided by rocks. Two are divided by a rocky peninsula, Le Castel, joined to the mainland by a strip of sand. Westerly winds make it a splendid place for sailing and in summer the bay is sprinkled with sails of many colours. You can take a boat to the isle of Millau, from which you can see a great stretch of the coast. There is a golf course.

One of my old favourites – a seaside hotel with lovely sea views and luscious sea food.

From Trébeurden along the coast to Trégastel (11km) and Perros-Guirec (7km further) is called the Rose Granite coast because masses of rose-red rocks divide the beaches and even pop up in fields. You have views of Île Grande and Les Sept Îles, you can take a boat around the Seven Isles from Perros-Guirec but only land on Monk Isle; the others are bird sanctuaries.

One of my favourite drives in Brittany is to take D65 to Lannion (9km), a river port with many old timbered houses like a set for a musical of old Brittany. Best houses are in place Général Leclerc and alleys leading off.

Take D786 to St Michel-en-Grève (18km on), charming tiny beach resort at the end of the magnificent Lieue de Grève beach (4km long). At St Efflam (chapel of Irish hermit and domed fountain) turn right on D42 then on to D64 round the Corniche de l'Armorique to Locquirec (15km from St Michel), a super little fishing port and resort with delightful walled harbour, sands and an old church belonging once to the Knights of St John. Walk round the point for some fine views. This coast is quite eccentric – very heavily indented. Continue on D64 to Lanmeur, then take a small road right, C4, to St Antoine and D76 beside the estuary of the Dossen river (often called the Morlaix river) to Morlaix. There is a huge viaduct across the estuary dominating this busy old town. Grand'Rue has some fine old houses and shops, and the museum of art and folklore in a fifteenth-century church has an old rose window and modern paintings.

I can still remember a meal I had here ten years ago, especially the supreme clams (palourdes) stuffed with shallots, cream, cheese and a touch of garlic. Since then a new Breton chef Jean-Yves Guégan has arrived but Danielle Jouanny is still in the kitchen with him and I hope to recall some of their dishes in another ten years. Jean-Yves is a superb sauce chef. But much of the secret of the continuing success of the hotel's reputation for excellent cooking is in the buying of local ingredients. Gérard Jouanny chooses meticulously the best products of local farms, markets and fishing boats, refusing anything which he thinks is not up to his standards. The result is that his plateau de fruits de mer, for instance, is outstanding even in a country where every kitchen prides itself on its seafood platter. One of his menus is simply this, followed by cheese and a delicious apple tart.

The cheapest menu has a smaller plate of fruits de mer among its choice of starters, but the choice is very difficult, for the hotel is known for its fish soup. There was fresh mackerel cooked in Aligoté white wine, and a speciality – terrine chaude aux deux poissons. This is mouth-watering and delicious, and I could not resist it.

Two mousses are made with salmon and pike. The fish is minced finely and mixed with egg and cream and cooked gently. Then alternate layers of each mousse are cooked in a bain marie for 1½ hours. It is sliced when cold, then warmed and served with beurre blanc (shallots poached in Muscadet and whipped with butter) and a crayfish sauce.

When we were there last, the main course was served with purée of carrot, baked potato coated with fines herbes (finely chopped parsley, chives, tarragon and chervil), and spinach baked in egg. There was delicate salmon in sorrel, pavé de boeuf sauce Choron (steak in a sauce of egg yolks, shallots, vinegar, wine and tarragon mixed with tomato purée – a sort of tomato Béarnaise), and chicken breasts in a sauce of cream and egg yolks (en blanquette). But here by the sea I went for pollack in red pepper sauce.

The cheese was served with home-made walnut bread. I love it.

The desserts included hot apple tart and a light and beautiful marquise of chocolates and raspberries.

The five-course, most expensive, menu has some dishes to tempt a fasting saint – salmon and pollock marinated in spices and served raw, langoustines baked in a garlicky tomato Provençal sauce, fillet of sole in truffled butter. And on the card at a reasonable price is grilled Breton lobster.

You will need to stay a fortnight to do justice to the cooking here. And many guests do.

The only possible white wine with that platter of seafood is one of the very best of all Muscadets, Château de l'Oiselinière, tasting of ripe grapes, not sharp ones. With the hot fish dishes, try Coteaux Champenois (still Champagne) Blanc de Blancs de Chardonnay at below-average price.

Considering this is cider country, with the nearest wines made around Nantes, there is a good list of reds, including a good and cheap Côtes de Ventoux from Vaucluse and a 1970 Laffite Rothschild. I was tempted by the 1976 Château Andron Blanquet St Estèphe. This bourgeois growth may not have the finesse of the top wines like Calon-Ségur but is robust, satisfying and has flavour – for a consumer rather than a connoisseur.

I missed until too late an interesting Bordeaux red on this list – one I have not met for years. It is a fifth growth Haut Médoc from very near Margaux called Château Cantemerle, and the 1964 costs much less than the 1967, which surprises me because all the experts say that this property produced better wine before 1967. A fifth growth (cinquième cru) wine of Bordeaux is certainly not to be despised. The top four crus are full of wines which most of us dream of drinking fairly regularly when we have won the pools. So a 1964 is obviously not cheap. But I reckon this one would be a pricey bargain to a winesman.

RELAIS DU
SILENCE

NORTH
EAST OF
PARIS

Aux Armes de Champagne

Aux Armes de Champagne
L'Épine, 51000 Châlons-sur-
Marne (8km E of Châlons on
N8).
Telephone: (26) 68.10.43.
Rooms B–E;
menus A (weekdays), B
(Champenois), D.
Closed 10 January to 15
February.
Visa, Euro, Diners.

*Jean-Paul Pérardel also owns
the Angleterra Hotel in Chalons
– where meals are just as good.
Hugues Houard cooked there
originally*

The little village of Épine has a big Flamboyant-Gothic church started in 1400, a shrine for pilgrims since the Hundred Years War, and fit to be a cathedral. Opposite stands a cathedral of gastronomy and a shrine for wine-lovers – the long, low, modern Aux Armes de Champagne. Started in 1907 as a café by the Pérardel family, who still run it, it grew over three generations into a three-star hotel, renowned restaurant and wine cave. Twenty years ago a fire virtually destroyed it. In its rebuilding, it lost some old rural character but gained enormously in comfort. And its most comfortable furnishings, immaculate table settings, its service and its beautiful garden with pools and streams take it way out of the class of a village hotel into what *Gault Millau* calls 'luxeuse auberge', and to which *Michelin* gives a star for cuisine.

Jean-Paul Pérardel believes in excellence. His wife Denise has fine taste in furnishing and décor and a gift for growing and arranging flowers, which are used profusely in decoration.

The bedrooms are elegant. The dining room, panelled in light wood, looks on to Notre Dame church which is floodlit at night. There is a pleasant bar (often lacking in the best French hotels) and the *cave* next door – Le Marché aux Vins, run by the Pérardel family. Here you can choose from hundreds of fine wines at most reasonable prices which ones you will take home – and they include sparkling and still Champagne from the Pérardel's own caves at Epernay.

That church opposite is truly majestic.

Food & Drink

Hugues Houard was chef at La Mère Poulard at Mont St Michel, famous in ancient days for Mother Poulard's omelettes, and after eight years at Aux Armes de Champagne must be tired of jokers asking for a quick omelette and chips. Perhaps that is why the card politely warns eaters that 'Fresh cooking takes time. Quality and speed do not always go together.' But he had a

LOCAL DRIVES *Châlons-sur-Marne (8km W on N3) is a big agricultural centre and industrial city in the middle of the Champagne plain, and crossed by the Marne and canals. Some Champagne is made there, but more beer. The star attraction is St Etienne cathedral with beautiful twelfth to thirteenth-century glass windows and a carillon of fifty-six bells. In AD 451, Attila the Hun, ('Scourge of God') was beaten here by the Francs, Romans and Visigoths, in a bloody battle in which 200,000 men died. He fled to Hungary and turned his hordes on Italy.*

Epernay (33km) – go by N3 north of the Marne, through the picturesque wine town of Ay, whose Champagne is particularly subtle and delicate. Wine was made here in Roman times and was the favourite of the great rivals Francis I of France and Henry VIII of England – all they had in common except a love of pomp, ostentation and women. To the right of the road before Ay is Bouzy, a village producing red grapes for Champagne and the great Bouzy still red wine which the locals keep to themselves. It is like a delicate but great Burgundy. For Reims, take N3, then right at Mareuil (another good Champagne village with a château), on to the white roads through the forest of the Mountain of Reims. For information on Reims cathedral and visits to its wine caves, see the entry under Hostellerie du Château, Fère-en-Tardenois, page 50.

good laugh this year when a seriously critical British guide said: 'the cook is an *ancien* of Mère Poulard but has picked up a lot of imaginative spicey new ideas since then.' Mère Poulard is hardly a pancake shop. It has three very well-known chefs, a *Michelin* star and is famous for its dishes based on lamb 'pré-salé' – from the sea-washed marshes.

Hugues Houard is worth his *Michelin* star and high ratings all round for his flexibility and inventiveness. He changes his menus and card so often according to season and market that it is a little difficult to recommend a definite meal. But we have never had a bad dish.

Weekdays, he has a good cheap meal – a typical menu would be: fillet of ling (fish called Julienne in France) with grapefruit or salad Niçoise; guinea fowl in ratafia (brandy with grape juice), or curried lamb; cheese or sorbet.

Study the menu Champenois. I had excellent Champagne escargots in cassolette, mouth-watering 'pièce de boeuf' (not any old 'piece of beef' but real top rump) cooked in Bouzy red wine and beef-marrow stock, with vegetables, choice of a fine platter of cheeses, and a superb local gâteau.

Hugues often serves in his five-course most expensive menu one of his very special dishes – saumon de beurre d'Échiré – salmon cutlet in the famous Poitou butter. That sounds simple enough. But the making of the butter sauce alone includes spinach, shallots, parsley, chervil, tarragon, chives, lemon juice, leaves of mint, spicey St Florentin cheese from Burgundy, Crème fraîche (slightly soured cream), and a glass of blanc de blancs Champagne. Other spendid dishes I would try are his ris de veau à l'orange et au avocat (veal sweetbreads in orange and avocado) and le foie gras chaud au sabayon au Champagne (hot foie gras pâté in a sort of zabaglione of frothed egg whites, cream and Champagne wine). The compulsory magret de canard (duck's breasts) of contemporary cuisine comes not with the usual raspberry vinegar but with various sauces, like traditional cider and crayfish, with a blackberry sauce, and with 'thé et cassis', which must be a masterstroke of oneupmanship. I thought that he might be pulling the leg of someone out there among the priests and pundits of Nouvelle Cuisine, but Barbara tells me it was delicious. I think 'thé' must mean something different in Nouvelle language, like hot juices or meat stock. The desserts are delicious. Try ice cream with nut and nougat.

The wine list is prodigious, a joy to the heart without emptying the wallet. Pérardel family Champagne at table is reasonably priced, the very good family still Champagne 'Blanc de Chardonnay' is ideal for any fish. Burgundies run from a drinkable Passetoutgrains to a 1966 Richebourg (it's years since I drank one; even if I could have afforded it, I have not seen it). Among more expensive wines, there are special offers of the month. That Richebourg was reduced by 110F while I was there – making it an expensive bargain.

To return to earth, I would definitely pick a red Bouzy with meat or fowl – Marguet Bonnerave or the 1976 Tornay Millesime (a deliciously subtle and easy-to-drink wine).

Ratafia de Champagne (brandy and grape juice) is a special house apéritif. The other is Crémant framboise (a sort of Kir Royale with Crémant Champagne and raspberry liqueur).

La Bannière de France

La Bannière de France
11 rue Franklin-Roosevelt,
Laon, 02000 Aisne.
Telephone: (23) 23.21.44.
Rooms A–E (include family
rooms for four;
menus A–D;
half-board C–E.
Closed 20 December to 10
January.

An old-style French inn rather than a luxury hotel, in a fairy-tale old city. One of my oldest favourites.

Laon is one of the gems of old France. A walled, medieval city high on a steep hill, it was capital of France during the Charlemagne dynasty (eighth to tenth centuries). Charlemagne's mother Berthe, 'Big Foot' was born nearby, and five kings lived here. The capital was moved to Paris in 987.

One of the newer buildings behind the ancient walls, not quite 300 years old, is the former coaching inn, La Bannière de France. It is not a luxury hotel. But it is snug and comfortable with nice old furniture, has a most friendly and welcoming atmosphere and serves food way above what you would expect at an inn. Its customers keep going back. Its hotel facilities rate only two stars, its restaurant a good three stars, but redecorating has made the bedrooms much more comfortable, plumbing has improved and the dining room has had a facelift and has Louis XV brocades and décor, though far too provincial for the extravagant tastes of Madame de Pompadour or Madame du Barry. Paul Lefèvre

and his wife are most helpful and 'gentils'.

It is a gentle short stroll from the front door to the twelfth-century cathedral with its seven towers and simply superb interior, and to the charming chapel of the Knights Templars, with a pleasant garden planted over the graves of Templars and their successors here, the Knights of St John. A nice gesture at the cathedral are effigies of oxen peeping from upper windows in honour of the beasts which pulled the blocks of stone up the steep hill.

There are pleasant walks alongside the medieval ramparts, with superb views over the newer town below to the countryside of the Champagne.

Food & Drink

Dominique Havot has cooked here for over ten years and I know people who will drive an extra hundred kilometres to eat here. All the cooking team have worked in major restaurants of Paris. The restaurant caters for

The beautiful forest of St Gobain is reached by N44 or D7. It is mainly of oaks and has drives passing through valleys and alongside shallow little lakes (étangs). A rewarding circuit, taking in the ruins of the old fortified abbey of La Tortoir, the town of St Gobain famous for glass manufacture since the time of Louis XIV, Roches de l'Ermitage where the Irish hermit St Gobain is said to have lived, and the ancient abbey of Prémontre, would cover 65 to 70km. The abbey was founded in the eleventh century by St Norbert who was riding along when a voice castigated him for his dissipation. The Norbertine Order once had 1500 abbeys and convents around Europe. Rebuilt in the eighteenth century, the abbey is now a psychiatric hospital and casual visitors are not welcome.

At Mont Crèpy, 10km along the N44, is the site of Germany's 'secret weapon' with which they hoped to win the war in 1918. Here stood Big Bertha, the massive gun which shelled Paris.

Reims is 58km away from Laon – for visiting the cathedral and wine caves (see Hostellerie du Château, Fère-en-Tardenois, page 50).

all pockets and most tastes, except the fanatics of classical heavy sauces or of Nouvelle Cuisine.

A remarkably cheap three-course menu has a choice of six dishes in each course, including the splendid vegetable soup, fresh-made daily, and chicken in white wine, and a quarter litre of red wine.

There are some really delicious, rather pricey specialities on the card, and some of them are often on the priciest, but not dear, menu as well. Outstanding among many good starters are the artichoke and langoustines salad and salade royale, a delightful mixture of scallops, crayfish and foie gras of duck.

If in a spending mood, I would follow the artichoke

salad with noix de St Jacques à l'avocat – scallops with avocado. The scallops are braised in oil, cream is added and the liquid reduced. Then white of leeks cooked in cream are stirred in. Finally skinned slices of avocado are added and everything reheated. It is superb.

Then I would choose between veal kidneys in a splendid sweet and sour sauce (rognons de veau à l'aigre-doux) and the not-too-rare magret de canard in Reinette apples and Calvados apple spirit – a true Normand dish, so to speak!

Normally I would settle for the excellent value menu of four courses, with a choice of four dishes on each course. My favourite starter is terrine de tourteaux au beurre Nantais – crab terrine with a white butter (beurre blanc) made from shallots cooked in Muscadet wine whipped into butter. Then I would go for rognons de veau au Bouzy – chopped veal kidneys are sautéed in oil, then the juices de-fatted and de-glazed with Bouzy, the still red wine of Champagne. Strong veal stock is added and the sauce reduced. Then foie gras is mixed with 'crème fraîche' (slightly soured cream) and stirred in with the kidneys. It is one of the best kidney dishes we know.

This is a good area for cheese – Arrigny, Carré de l'Est, Chaources, lovely soft creamy Coulomniers, Les Ricey Cendré (a flat, round ash-coated cheese tasting almost fruity) and Barbéry (soft cheese cured in ashes). You will find a good selection on the cheeseboard.

La Bannière's desserts are rightly praised by the *Gault Millau* guide. The pâtisserie and chocolate profiteroles (éclairs) are quite outstanding.

La Bannière's cellars have a fine choice of Bordeaux red wines, from a Château Melone 1979 at a most reasonable price to a first growth Château Latour. Any would go nicely with the kidneys or duck. My choice at lower prices would be the 1975 Château Lagrosse, a première Côte de Bordeaux.

The Bouzy red wine of Champagne is like a delicious but soft Burgundy, is produced in small quantities which the locals like to keep for themselves, and is always rather dear. If you want to try a good one, now is your chance – a 1980 Georges Vesselles. It would also be logical to try a Coteaux Champenois, a still dry white, with the fish. A Pol Roger Blanc de Blancs is on the list, and although I love it, as I do Bouzy, my bank manager would definitely prefer me to stick to the 1981 Muscadet sur lie, which is a good one (Domaine du Bois Bruley) and good value.

Among his sixteen bubbly Champagnes, Paul Lefèvre recommends his Blanc de Blancs Crémant brut 1974 from Abel Lipitre in Reims. It is certainly dry, fruity and refreshing, and Crémant wines, being somewhat less bubbly, don't make you sneeze when you laugh.

In Champagne, blanc de blancs means wine made entirely from Chardonnay grapes, not mixed with Pinot noir. It is usually lighter, and Jacques Mercier told me that he found it ideal for drinking at 11a.m. – or perhaps breakfast.

Château de Bellinglise Elincourt-Sainte-Marguerite, 60157 Oise (on D142 between Lassigny and its junction with N32 near Compiègne (15km); or leave A1 motorway at Ressons, drive through Margny).
Telephone: (4) 476.04.76.
Rooms F–G;
menus A, B, C, D;
half-pension F.
Closed Sunday evenings, Mondays.
Visa, Euro, Diners.

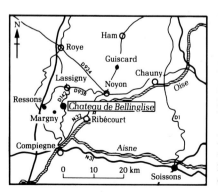

This formidable fifteenth-century castle leads a double life. In the huge old red-bricked château, reflected across lawns in a big lake amid 650 acres of woodland, are large old bedrooms with beautiful antique furnishings. Half a mile away, deep in the woods, are little modern *pavillons* of comfortable, bright modern bedrooms decorated with flowery wallpaper.

The old castle has a maze of rooms. If you open a strange door you are likely to find groups of people sitting round tables in earnest conference, or a wedding or birthday party eating, drinking and generally jollificating. When I was there on a Saturday night, I was drawn after dinner into a birthday dance which seemed to spread to all the guests. But these groups drink and dine separately and the individual guests can live in peace and tranquillity.

There are so many rooms that Madame Pollet, wife of the owner, Roger, is still searching for antiques to complete some of the decor. Most older bed-rooms have huge beds, ample wardrobes, chests and chairs, and room for love-seats and even settees.

The bar-lounge is delightful, with very comfortable chairs and settees around a log fire. Another log fire burns in the elegant dining room, beneath a marble mantelpiece, a superb ornate brass clock and a picture of a breasty eighteenth-century beauty. Full panelling, an old chandelier and delightful chairs add to the feeling of comfort. Tables are impeccably laid on purest white linen.

You can fish in the lake among water lilies, or play tennis. The walks through the woods and to the surrounding villages are delightful. The *pavillons* are built on a track-road among a few private houses – modern and individual. Most of these belong to pilots of various nationalities from Charles de Gaulle airport – some are bachelors. Combined with young couples who drive down the motorway from Paris (96km) or Belgium, they add a little pleasant liveliness to a remote spot. The hotel is cheaper than you would expect from a Château Hotel Independent of this standard.

Food & Drink

One of chef Luc Macaigne's three top specialities is magret de canard au vinaigre de framboises – half-cooked duck breasts in raspberry vinegar, which is the symbol of Nouvelle Cuisine and one of my unfavourite dishes. But I don't have to choose it, and I shall forgive him because he produces a canard Vallée d'Auge (in Calvados, cider and cream) which is delightful.

The cheapest menu is good value. The starters last time I was there included gorgeous Bayonne jambon cru (ham mildly smoked and cured in wine), and the main course choices were pork chop or escalope of young turkey (dindonneau). The second cheapest menu was excellent value, with melting ficelle Picarde as starter (pancake stuffed with cream and ham). One alternative was a pancake stuffed with mixed shellfish. Among main course choices were steak archiduc (with paprika and cream) and côte de veau Ardennaise (veal chop cooked with juniper berries) which I found excellent.

But one meal of the third menu showed me that it was worth the extra francs. Missing the chef's speciality of snails, and his other of supreme of turbot au Champagne, I chose filet de sole Duglère. This is named after one of the best Paris chefs of the eighteenth

Compiègne (15km) – a pleasant riverside town, rich in art and history. Joan of Arc was imprisoned here before she went to the stake. With the beautiful forest alongside it was always a royal hunting centre. Louis XIV was there often, 'living like a peasant' at his hunting lodge, but Louis XV ordered its rebuilding in 1738. Louis XVI finished it as a château. It became a military school after the Revolution, then Napoleon I moved in. His furnishings remind us that he was not a man of artistic flair.

The place started to swing when Napoleon III and Empress Eugénie moved in. They loved it, and held hunts, balls, theatricals and parties here. The museum of their furnishings is more interesting. The Vivenel Museum has some superb Greek vases. Musée de la Figurine has 80,000 wood, board and lead toy soldiers. Most interesting to me is the transport museum, created by the Touring Club de France. It has a wonderful selection of vehicles from the eighteenth-century onwards.

Drive on by N31, then D546 through Compiègne forest to a railway carriage in a clearing (Clairière de l'Armistice), replica of the coach where the Germans surrendered in 1918, and the French to Hitler in 1940. At Blérancourt there is a very interesting museum of Franco-American Friendship in the château.

century. The fish is cooked in wine and stock with tomatoes, onions, parsley and cream. Luc Macaigne cooks it superbly, adding a few little slices of mushroom. It melted with the most subtle flavour for such simple ingredients. After this course I was served a sorbet of Marc – which I favour.

The duck Vallée d'Auge was cooked as I like it. I do not like duck cooked too little so that it is rubbery, however good the flavour. A true Vallée d'Auge sauce should surely have had more cream, but there is a fashion now to use the valley's name for many sauces containing cider or Calvados, and I certainly have no complaints about Luc's sauce.

There was a salad, a good cheeseboard and for dessert I chose bavarois au cassis – thick egg and whipped cream custard flavoured with blackcurrant – which is unusual and very nice.

It was an excellent meal. A little more imagination in the meat dishes would have made it even better.

The wine list shows imagination, reasonable prices and a fair all round choice. With my duck I had a good 1976 Château Jean Faure. This is a grand cru – a great wine of St Emilion,

just heavy enough to go well with fowl or game, and good value. There were several good Bordeaux wines, including a Château Bosque St Estephe 1975 and a Château Mont Bousquet Medoc. You can pay a lot for the very best of St Emilion, Cheval Blanc, which is red and pure nectar.

With the sole, I treated myself to a half bottle of a good Chablis, for the price of a whole bottle of a Sevre et Maine Muscadet sur lie – left to lie on its 'lie' (pips and skin or must) for a long time to give it extra strength and flavour. A good Sancerre here costs less than average prices these days.

My aperitif Kir was made with Aligoté wine and crème de cassis. The inventor, Canon Kir, would have approved. He used Aligoté. But he would not have approved of his name being mis-spelt (Kirr) on a bar notice urging you to drink it. The good Canon was churchman in Dijon, resistance leader against the Nazis, then Mayor, and to help local blackcurrant juice (cassis) and wine producers, he invented this drink and served it always at mayoral functions. It became fashionable on the Riviera – and still is.

Outstanding value for satisfying, well-cooked meals

Le Château de Ligny

Château de Ligny
59191 Ligny Haucourt, nr Caudry, Nord (N43 SE from Cambrai to Beauvois-en-Cambresis, then right on D74). Telephone: (27) 85.25.84. Rooms G, apartments H; menus D, F(gourmet). Closed: hotel January; Mondays, Tuesday mornings November to Easter; restaurant also closed Monday lunch Easter to November. Visa.

A member of Châteaux Hôtels de France, and expensive. But the patron of this thirteenth-century château, André Blot, says that a stay here is a festive occasion, and he is right.

It is an interesting and seductive place. The castle is built round a courtyard, and has a round bell tower with six-sided pointed roof. Around the walls are a small park where fallow deer graze, and a garden with a pond and fountain and chairs and tables under a magnolia tree. We had a luxurious and very pricey apartment with two rooms furnished in a mixture of antique and modern furniture which blended surprisingly well. The whole apartment was close carpeted in white, including the bathroom, which had two wash basins, a covered sink, electric ring for tea making, a fridge with soft drinks, and a double width bath. True togetherness.

The dining room is the old armoury, with large stone fireplace for burning logs. You dine by candlelight. Through a grill in the floor you can see a tunnel, lit up. A bit of a mystery. It is believed that once it led to the church but then became a dungeon for prisoners.

The tower is the part of the castle dating from the thirteenth century or before. The rest of the castle was built in the fifteenth century in Flemish Renaissance style.

The moat has been filled in. In 1917, occupying Germans discovered firing steps used by archers and later walled up, and in the cellars graffiti and coats of arms.

Mme Catherine de Staal, new Maîtresse de Maison, is charming and most efficient.

Food & Drink

There are some delightful dishes to taste. The menu is good but does not have both a fish and meat course, and the gourmet menu, which does have both, plus a sorbet digestive in the middle, has magret de canard as its main course, so I would go for the card. After all, it is a festive occasion.

Among the starters are mussels in fennel, a home-made

foie gras of duck which is obviously more expensive and a flamiche picarde. Well made, as it is here, this dish of the Flemish peasants is a joy. It is a leek, cheese and cream tart, rather Devonian. On the fish course, sandre is the house speciality, baked in foil. It is a delicate fish, a cross between pike and perch, but with more flavour. It used to be fairly rare but turns up on many menus these days like trout in Britain; I suspect it may be farmed. My choice is the mille feuilles aux deux saumons panachés – smoked and fresh salmon and salmon roe in a flakey pastry – a delicious dish which I shall try making at home. It was served with slices of courgettes, carrots and avocado. Not wishing to eat two lots of pastry, Barbara skipped the flamiche and had fresh asparagus in a mousseline sauce – butter, egg yolks and lemon juice in wine, like a hollandaise sauce, but lightened with whipped cream.

Barbara missed the main course, and so missed ris de veau aux langoustines – sweetbreads in a sauce with prawns. You can have grilled goat cheese on salad, which I love, or a choice of an outstandingly interesting cheeseboard, which includes five goats' cheeses and several strong local cheeses: Maroilles, supple creamy cheese with strong smell and taste invented in the tenth century at the Maroilles monastery and now made by farmers; a herb and pepper flavoured Maroilles called Dauphin after Louis XIV's son; Boulette d'Avesnes, another strong-smelling and tasting soft cheese flavoured with herbs, with a red rind; Boulette de Cambrai, a milder herb-flavoured cheese made in farms and homes around here; Le vieux Lille, called often Gris de Lille, like Maroilles but cured in brine and beer, very strong smelling and sometimes also called Puant de Lille 'stinking of Lille'. Lovely! A splendid place for cheese tasting, with a nice strong red wine with body.

Desserts are a speciality, too. Top comes Barbara's favourite – Symphonie Royale (simply raspberry sorbet surrounded by fresh fruit, in our case à rouge – raspberries, strawberries and red cherries). For me, marquise au chocolat, crème menthe – a chocolate sponge which melts in your mouth, rolled with whipped cream flavoured with mint. Marquise is the only chocolate dessert I like.

Breakfast is good with three home-made jams, but, alas, instead of croissant, a sticky bun.

LOCAL DRIVES

Cambrai (17km) was badly damaged in both World Wars, but many of its treasures remain; bypassed now by motorways. Fine linen, 'cambric', mentioned by Shakespeare, is still made there. It is also the home of andouillette, the coarse sausage of pork guts, and of tripe. But St Géry church is more interesting. It has a 250-foot (76- metre) high belfry, a Renaissance rood screen, and twelve large paintings, including the enormous 'Entombment' by Rubens. In the municipal museum are a good collection of Dutch and Flemish paintings and also works by Utrillo, Ingres, Boudin and Vlaminck, and sculpture by Rodin and Bourdelle.

The Forest of Mormal (D74 to Beauvois on N43, right to Le Cateau, D969 to Landrecies, small road into forest, 35km) is a charming forest of oaks and beech, much cut down by the German army in 1917 but since recovered. The biggest forest in the north of France, and important industrially, it is a lovely spot for walking among hills and valleys, driving round 55km of foresters' roads for picnics and rest. One nice little village, Locquignol, once a centre of wood sculptors and clog makers (sabotiers), has a good inn – La Touraille.

Le Cateau was the birthplace of Matisse, the Impressionist painter (1869–1954). There is a museum of his drawings, gravures, sculptures and tapestries.

Such a feast deserves the best wines. There are plenty. There are two house aperitifs – La Vierge Rose (Champagne and strawberry liqueur – very suitable for virgins) and Le Sire de Ligny (white wine and peach juice). I was more tempted by the reasonably-priced Réserve du Château, a white dry Graves served in magnums!

There is a very good choice of wines at all prices and not overpriced for a Château hotel. As I was having two first courses with pastry involved, I changed my habit of drinking Sancerre or Muscadet first and settled for one of our favourite Chablis – the Premier Cru Fourchaume produced by Gérard Tremblay at Domaine des Isles. It is beautifully balanced.

There is a fine choice of red Bordeaux for the main course, and if you are really 'en fête' you could choose a delicious rich, subtle Château Smith-Haut-Laffite 1976 Graves from Martillac. I know that it sounds like a joke name but it is one of the true cru classé reds of Graves, and they are usually better than the white Graves. Not quite so good because still a little young, but one of my favourites, is the 1980 Château de Brane Cantenac, cheaper than the Graves. It is one of the biggest Margaux vineyards and Lucian Lurton is a very skilled producer. I am leaving the 1980 which I have for a few more years. There is a superb 1975 Château Grand Corbin St Emilion at a price. For something cheaper try 1979 Clos des Templiers, not a true Pomerol but a neighbouring appellation, Lalande-de-Pomerol, and surprisingly luscious. Or Les

Vieux Rocs Lussac-St Emilion is good value – fruity but not sharp. This would go with the strong local cheeses, too. But I should be tempted to buy a separate bottle for them – the cheapest bottle on the list, strong, strong-tasting Chateâu de Parusc Cahors. I did see some optimist taking a Bandol rosé with these cheeses. Oh, dear. The cheese must have murdered it.

If you are having a festive occasion with a loving companion, don't forget to order the Champagne with your breakfast in bed.

The first - or last taste of France for a luxury-loving gourmet.

HOSTELLERIE DU CHATEAU ★★★★

**Hostellerie du Château
Fère-en-Tardenois, 02130
Aisne.
Telephone: (23) 82.21.23.
Rooms G–H but one meal
must be taken;
menus D, E:
Closed January, February.
Visa, Euro, Amex.**

If I wanted to impress a sophisticated, much travelled lady, I would take her to this château hotel. It is magnificent; quite one of the best hotels in Europe. And appropriately priced, of course, although you would not get such good taste, service and atmosphere for anywhere near the price outside France, nor would you get the same cooking.

The antique furniture is almost perfectly appropriate to each room. The décor is comfortable, soothing and French, with flowery silk wall hangings in some rooms.

The dining room is furnished with true elegance. All the tableware from cutlery and crockery to silver and linen is perfect. Service is formal and almost too faultless, but Gérard Blot, his wife and two sisters bring courteous friendliness. And the cooking is superb.

All this in a marvellous stone château, part Renaissance, in a big park of lawns, flower beds and copses, with the original castle ruin alongside. You reach it by a long, climbing drive from N367, 3km outside

the little town of Fère-en-Tardenois, in the heart of the quiet countryside yet only a few miles north of the A4 Paris-Reims motorway (leave it at Château-Thierry or Dormans). Château-Thierry is 22km on the N367, Soissons 26km on the D4.

The first château was built in 1206. Francis I gave it to his immensely rich and powerful Constable of France, Anne de Montmorencey (a man), in 1528. His descendant Henry II was executed for opposing Richelieu (my ancestors were more cunning and got away to England). The castle was given to the Prince of Condé. It came later to Louis Philippe, Duke of Orleans, gambler, lover of women, friend of our own Prince Regent, who popularized the old English sports of horse-racing and hard-drinking in France, gave away a lot to the poor, joined the Revolutionaries, called himself Philippe Egalité, became a Deputy for Paris, voted for the execution of the King, and knocked down part of his Fère château to show how 'equal' he was. He was still guillotined because his son deserted to the Austrians. Ironically, his son, after living in Twickenham, became King Louis-Philippe of France, the 'citizen-king'. The citizens got tired of him and he fled to England as 'Mr Smith'. Happily, the château was mostly restored in the last century.

Food & Drink

Even the *most* sophisticated and travelled lady would be impressed by the Château cuisine. *Michelin* gives it two stars, *Gault* guide says 'better and better'. Young Patrick Michelon is becoming one of France's best chefs, and the young pâtissier is worth his weight in gold to Gérard Blot. The desserts are delightful.

You must forget calories and bank accounts at the Château. The first menu is very good but lacks choice. To woo that sophisticated lady pick the more expensive Dégustation, or something from the card.

The first menu when I was there started with gâteau de foie blond aux écrevisses – pounded chicken livers mixed with foie gras, eggs, truffle juice and cream, steamed and served with crayfish sauce. I would choose it from the card, anyway. There followed a fresh shellfish salad, marée du jour (what the tide brought in). Then a welcome digestive – sorbet en Marc, the spirit distilled from grape skins, pips and stalks after wine pressing.

The main course was lamb noisette in estragon (tarragon to us). The cheeseboard is immaculate – inevitably strong in Brie and local Thierry cheeses. You can choose your dessert from the list, including the trolley, with simply delicious inventions – light, pretty and melting. In the Dégustation menu you can choose two desserts. See what I mean about calories?

If you go nap on the card and blow the expense, an alternative to the foie blond for me would be the platette d'huitres chaudes (hot oysters in rice, peppers and beetroot). My fish course would have to be the

Paris 108km. Laon (49km) – lovely hilltop medieval city with rampart walks, fine views, a superb twelfth-century cathedral; it was capital of France before Paris (see Bannière de France, Laon, page 41). Drive on from Laon through the charming forest of St Gobain to Blérancourt (its château has a fascinating Franco-American museum, including a Ford T-model ambulance from the First World War). On to the clearing in the forest where in the First World War Armistice was signed in a railway carriage and Hitler insisted upon taking the French surrender in 1940. Then to Compiègne (55km from Fère) along Route Eugénie through the oak and beech forest – a lovely drive. The old royal castle at Compiègne contains many treasures. (See Château de Bellinglise, Elincourt St Marguerite, page 44.)

Reims-Epernay – Reims (46km) suffered terribly in the First World War, and the incomparable cathedral was damaged. Its rebuilding was a symbol for France. Started in 1211, not finished until the fifteenth century, shattered and burned by revolutions and wars, it stands almost as it did when Joan of Arc persuaded her beloved, timid and unwilling Dauphin to be crowned there as Charles VII. It is a masterpiece of harmony and symmetry, with superb ornamental Gothic sculptures.

Find out about wine cellars from Comité Inter Professionel du Vin de Champagne, 5 rue Henri-Martin, 51200 Epernay (telephone: (26) 51.40.47). In Reims, two that are open to the public without introduction are: Mumm, 34 rue du Champ de Mars, and Veuve Cliquot-Ponsadin, place des Droits de l'Homme. But Moët et Chandon in Epernay is a favourite for visits (20 ave Champagne; telephone: (26) 51.71.11).

chef's delicate turbot de petits bateaux au vieux Champagne maderisé – turbot poached in Champagne so old that it has become brown and oxidized, like a Madeira, with stock, tomatoes, shallots, garlic and mushrooms, with cream and parsley added to the reduced sauce.

On the main course the Château is known for its partridge, venison and hare in season, and for roast pigeon (pigeonneau), often with fèves des Marais (broad beans of Marais). I do not think pigeon roasts, even at the Château. Too often it goes hard and dry. I would choose dégustation des trois mignons – succulent fillets of veal, lamb and beef.

With cheese and a dessert, my choice would be costly – I did say, 'Blow the expense'.

Everything is beautifully decorated and presented.

I could save a little on the wines. There are Fleurie, Morgon or Brouilly from Beaujolais and a pleasant white Burgundy by Chauvet. Or cheaper Gamay, Beaujolais Villages and Loire Sauvignon. But having gone this far I would choose a Crémant Champagne – not quite so bubbly as Champagne. Then I would have the only still red of Champagne, Bouzy, to suit my meat and cheese courses. I love it and so little is made almost none leaves the area of France.

Yes, it costs a lot to eat at the Château. But it's a splendid experience.

One of the best hotels in the world.

CARTE DES QUATRE SAISONS

ENTRÉES

SALADE DE CRUSTACES A L'HUILE DE TRUFFES (homards - langoustines)	130.00
PALETTE D HUITRES CHAUDES	80.00
POTAGE AU GOUT DU JOUR	45.00
FOIE DE CANARD CHAUD A LA CROQUE AU SEL	85.00
PÂTÉ DU JOUR EN SALADE TIÈDE	70.00
FOIE GRAS D OIE DES LANDES AU NATUREL	100.00
SOUPE DE SAINT JACQUES AUX ASPERGES VERTES	80.00
GATEAU DE FOIE BLOND AUX ECREVISSES (essence de truffes)	60.00
CHARTREUSE DE VENAISON (PERDREAU, FAISAN, FOIE GRAS, sur melée de salade aux noix et reinettes)	90.00

POISSONS ET CRUSTACÉS

TURBOT DE PETITS BATEAUX EN ECAILLE DE CRUSTACES	140.00
HOMARD BRETON DE NOS VIVIERS - BEURRE DE CORAIL	200.00
BAR DE LIGNE AU BEURRE DE TRUFFES DE RICHERENCHES	100.00
FLAN DE CRESSON DANS UNE NAGE DE COQUILLAGES	70.00
DUO DE ST JACQUES ET LANGOUSTINES - PASSION DE LISE (vinaigrette tiède à l'huile de truffe)	90.00
TURBOTIN AU VELOUTÉ DE LEGUMES ROUGES	75.00
DAUBE DE HOMARD ET D HUITRES AU VIN DE LUDES	200.00
TRUITE DE MER SAUMONEE AU BEURRE DE VENUS	80.00
FILET DE SOLE AUX ECREVISSES	90.00

ROTS ET DORURES

PIGEONNEAU DU BOCAGE VENDEEN, ROTI AU MAIS	90.00
DEGUSTATION DES TROIS MIGNONS (FILET DE VEAU - AGNEAU - BOEUF)	90.00
POELE DE ROGNON ET RIS DE VEAU SUR LIT DE PERSIL	90.00
FILET DE BOEUF AU BOUZY	80.00
AIGUILLETTE DE CANARD CHALLANDAIS A L AIGRE DOUX (2 PERS.)	160.00
FILET D'AGNEAU ROTI EN SAVARIN SAUCE CRESSONNETTE	85.00
	120.00

LOIRE,
DORDOGNE
AND SOUTH
WEST

Hôtel Arcé

**Hôtel Arcé,
St Étienne-de-Baïgorry, 64430
Pyrénées-Atlantique. (On
D948, off D918 Bayonne-St
Jean Pied-de-Port).
Telephone: (59) 37.40.14.
Rooms D, E;
menus B, C:
half-board C–E.
Closed 2 November to 2
March.
Amex.**

*Take good walking shoes
and, of course, your fishing
rod to catch your own
trout for lunch.*

In the early 1950s when I was researching magazine articles about smuggling between France and Spain I stopped in the village of St Étienne-de-Baïgorry, 5km from the Spanish border. I wanted lunch. I found the Hotel-Restaurant Le Trinquet run by the Arcé family for four generations, with young Emile Arcé in the kitchen. On the tree-shaded terrace overlooking an arm of the river Nive I had a fine meal of Basque dishes and plenty of red wine.

Since then, the hotel has become known as the Arcé, has collected a *Michelin* star, and young Pascal Arcé (fifth generation, aged 24) has joined his father Emile in the kitchen. Otherwise, the river jumping with trout still hurries past the front door, the Pyrenees stand guard at the back door and a customs patrol stopped me down a little road, 10km from the frontier, to see what I was smuggling from Spain.

It is an unsophisticated hotel, comfortable but not luxurious, with old-fashioned décor, old-fashioned willing, friendly service, still the same Basque regional dishes despite gastronomic accolades, and is the sort of place I love.

Some of the local tracks which used to be called 'jeepable' are now tarmac, and the roads to Biarritz, 50km away at the seaside, and to St Jean Pied-de-Port the other way have been widened in places to take as many as three lorries abreast. You can find Basque folklorique dancing and singing and exhibition games of la pelote, a near lethal game like squash played with baskets strapped to the arms, arranged for tourists at St Jean (11km). But mostly St Etienne offers 'vacances calmes, reposantes et heureuses', as the Hotel Arcé brochure claims, and guests go for walks in the mountains, or into the thick woods, go fishing, or just sit and watch the fish dart around busily.

Bedrooms are cosy, all have bath or shower rooms, some have balconies overlooking the river and rooftops of the old village.

Go over the Spanish border to the bull-running town of Pamplona (75km) and seaside city of San Sebastian.

Bayonne (55km) – French Basque capital is very busy but still attractive, with a fine cathedral and a museum of Basque culture. Its ramparts are now gardens. Known for its cured ham, chocolates, salmon from the Adour river, Armagnac and Izarra (liqueur like Chartreuse – green and yellow), Bayonne became English when Eleanor of Aquitaine married Henry II, and stayed so for three centuries. Basque ships fought alongside our Navy. But it was the last place in France to hold out against Wellington. Biarritz is 8km away, once an elegant resort for the rich, now more popular, a bit faded and the capital of surfing in Europe. The Palace Hotel was a palace built by Napoleon III for his Empress Eugénie so that she could be near her beloved Spain.

St Jean-de-Luz (66km) – an interesting resort and fishing port; biggest tuna fishing fleet in France; Ciboure, 1km over the river, is the best place to eat fish, with daily quayside market and many restaurants cooking and serving it.

Cambo les Bains lower town (22km) by the river Nive is an attractive old Basque village. Ask the Arcé family about the lovely riverside, woodland and mountain drives around here. They speak English, by the way.

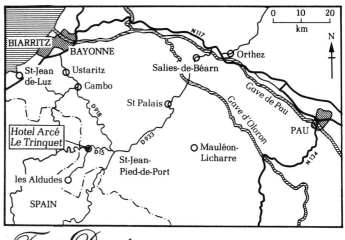

Food & Drink

I have always loved Basque cooking, but, like Catalan, it is easy to botch up in a hurry, difficult to do really well.

Pipérade, for instance: quite reputable British cookbooks describe it basically as scrambled eggs with peppers and vegetables added. It is sweet red peppers, onions, and tomatoes, sautéed in pork fat, with a touch of marjoram. Eggs are added at the end. The effect should be creamy with the red pepper flavour winning. The Arcé makes it beautifully.

Garbure, the Basque soup-stew, has many recipes, with each chef backing his own formula passionately. Usually it has a small joint of bacon, many different vegetables, sweet peppers, paprika, marjoram, thyme, and, of course, garlic, white cabbage cut in strips and confit of goose, duck or pork. Sometimes sausages and haricot beans are used. The Arcé serves a splendid version, with little sausages, on its menu simple (offering garbure,

the plat du jour, salad and dessert) and on its card.

Being near the Adour, the hotel buys really fresh salmon and sensibly serves it grilled. Grilled or poached in a court-bouillon is the way to serve it. Being 50km from the sea, the hotel buys splendid salmon trout and, cooked with almonds, it is excellent.

The Arcé has some delicious main courses, too – a home-produced confit of goose, lamb of the Pyrenees sautéed in paprika, and, in season (autumn, when the wild berries and nuts are plentiful), salmis de palombes. Palombes is a local wild pigeon.

Civet de Marcassin is on the card, too – jugged young boar. But the real local dish is truite au bleu – trout caught in the river alongside the hotel, plunged into a boiling wine and vinegar court-bouillon of herbs and vegetables to keep its absolutely fresh flavour. This turns the skin slightly blue. In these days of trout farms, it is rare to find wild trout simply and freshly cooked on a menu.

We begin to forget how delicious trout can be.

There are some splendid mountain cheeses served here, including Oloron (or Larrun), a goat's milk cheese best between October and May, and Poustagnac, fresh cow cheese flavoured with sweet peppers.

There are some good Bordeaux wines on the list, but you have a chance here to try a good, cheap local wine – Irouléguy. It is truly local, with just 100 acres of vines and all the wine produced in the village cooperative *caves*. There is a little white, a rosé with the exhortation on the label '*Hotx, Hotx, Edan*' (which is Basque for 'serve chilled', not hot), and a good sturdy red which I thought went very well with the garbure.

For a better red, try Madiran if Emile still has any. It is strong, has an appelation contrôlée, and is not easy to get. The best I have tasted is Rôt de Roy.

Jurançon white wines from south of Pau are delicious – dry or sweet (*moelleux*). I find the dry full of flowery flavour and body and suitable to drink with a wider range of dishes than such wines as Muscadet or Sancerre. The sweet wine has been cherished in France since Henry IV became addicted and is still underrated, despite setbacks from disease. A wine strong in perfume, flavour and alcohol (thirteen per cent), light coloured when young, tasting of honey and nuts, amber when aged, tasting of spices, especially nutmeg. A wine for all seasons and any time from elevenses until dinner dessert. The Arcé recommends it.

Hôtel Belle-Rive
Najac, 12270 Aveyron (from Villefranche de Rouergue, 59km E of Cahors, take D122n to La Fouillade 19km, right along D39 for 7km).
Telephone: (65) 65.74.20.
Rooms A–C;
menus A, B, C;
half-board B, C.
Closed 15 October to 1 April.

Escape to peace and beauty – a logis de France, with a 'casserole' for great regional cooking.

Connoisseurs' country, known to few Frenchmen. Above the river Aveyron valley where Quercy meets the Rouergue, it is a silent, sparsely populated land of steep hills, thick woods, some high plains, and narrow rough roads leading to very simple hamlets, some deserted. Tourists come to see the Gorges de l'Aveyron and especially the medieval hilltop town of Najac and its ruined castle. There is good fishing, too.

I have known Belle Rive since the early sixties and I am very fond of it. It is a fairly simple and reasonably comfortable country hotel where the cooking is well above average for the style of hotel and far above average for the price charged.

Bedrooms are comfortable, if a little uninspired, and all thirty-nine have perfectly good bathrooms. My bedroom last time looked on to a grassy bank, but the front rooms have a pleasing view over the river valley, and the lullaby of water burbling over a weir below. There is a bar, a pleasant rustic dining room with checked table cloths, and plenty of sitting room. The tree-shaded terrace looking over the river valley is big and delightful, and meals there in good weather are most enjoyable.

The service by friendly and smiling girls is delightful, too.

Surprisingly, behind the hotel, beneath a tree-covered slope topped by the château ruin, is an inviting swimming pool.

It is a peaceful hotel without being dead, and fine for scenic walks, fishing and horse riding.

Najac is a dramatic little town, its houses climbing up steep slopes to a narrow ridge jutting out in a spur. Below, the river Aveyron loops round the spur through a steep ravine, and it is just after the little bridge over it that you find the Belle-Rive hotel. The ruins of the thirteenth-century château stand on the highest point of the ridge. The view from the donjon tower, plunging dizzily to the river on three sides, is not for those with vertigo.

LOCAL DRIVES

Gorges de l'Aveyron; not dangerous driving but winding and quite hard work. There are fine views. Take D39 to just before La Lande, turn left on D638 over the river and railway to Monteils (chapel of a convent, with modern stained glass by Gustave Singier). Take D47 at the end of Monteils, left again on D149. Where it branches, take an unmade road on the left to the abandoned village of Courbières, with its lovely views over the river valley from the old castle. Then D149, D39 to Najac.

For Laguépie (16km) and Cordes (27km) take D239 uphill, with good views of the town and castle. The road winds snakily between wooded hills and over La Sérène river. Right on D122n to Laguépie, a charming village at the meeting of Aveyron and Viaur rivers. D122 to Cordes, known as Cordes-sur-Ciel because it stands 'in the sky' high on a spur overlooking the Cérou valley. Built by the Counts of Toulouse as a defence against Montfort's rampaging army, it has two oval ramparts. Climb the stairs to the top of the church tower and you will see superb views of the hills and valleys and see why this was a defence watch tower. Prosperous in the middle ages, the town was hit by religious wars and the plague, and was nearly abandoned when discovered in the 1940s by a painter, Yves Brayer, who founded a community of artists and craftsmen to restore it. The steep Grand'Rue leads to fine medieval houses, including the Huntsman's House with sculpted hunting scenes, and the Falconer's House.

Villefranche-de-Rouergue (24km N) was built as a bastide (fortified village) in the thirteenth century. Its cobbled, sloping market square is surrounded by ancient arcades and a huge church tower. Across the river on the Albi road is the fifteenth-century Chartreuse de St Sauveur, serving as alms houses since before the French Revolution. An interesting and attractive town.

Food & Drink

Jacques Mazières, who has taken over from his father, is a very good chef, and all four of his menus, but particularly the two cheaper ones, are remarkable value for such cooking in a country hotel like this.

The Rouergue is a good area for ham and pork sausages in various sizes and forms, for foie gras of duck and confits of goose, and superb trout and crayfish from the Aveyron river. Chicken is prepared in many of the classic ways and, of course, this is the land of Roquefort, the blue sheep's cheese matured in caves kept humid by an underground lake. Another local dish is tripous du Rouergue – lamb's tripe cooked in wine, tomatoes and ham. It is on the card. Not to my taste, however.

When I was last at the Belle-Rive, the very cheap menu offered an assortment of the local charcuterie, veal in cream, wine and mushroom sauce, which was excellent, served with gratin Dauphinois potatoes, which I love; then a choice of cheese and of dessert.

On the next menu, I had a most effective salad of lettuce and carrot turned in just the right amount of walnut oil and vinegar, liberally covered with grated Roquefort cheese and served with hot fried croutons of bread. Then there was a choice of salmon or trout from the river below. I chose trout, which had a very good flavour but was a little overdone. For the main course I chose coq au vin de Gaillac. Nouvelle snobbery has, alas, driven coq au vin off most ambitious menus.

You find it in cheaper restaurants. This one was tender and full of flavour, and was served with gratin Dauphinois. Roquefort cheese followed.

Desserts were not for slimmers – cream with almost everything. I saw two slim young ladies tucking into a large portion of chocolate gâteau with cream puffs. I had apple and blackcurrant sorbets with bilberries, Chantilly cream and crème de Cassis (blackcurrant liqueur).

It is all excellent regional cooking.

There is a wide choice of cheap wines to go with all this, mostly local or near local, plus a short list of Burgundy, Bordeaux and Rhône at below-average prices.

The Gaillac wines are from the Albert's Domaine de Labarthe and the Côtes du Tarn blanc sec is so fresh that I have heard it compared to spring water. I could do with a spring like that in my garden. In fact, these wines have a strong bouquet and a strong fruity taste, but little acidity.

I am not very fond of Gaillac reds, which are usually a bit thin and light. Belle-Rive has a very good, rather mysterious 1978 Cahors called Millesimme Exceptionnel. The vintage *was* exceptional and I recommend you to try it, if there is any left.

Among the more expensive Bordeaux wines, but still well below the price usually asked these days in restaurants, is a fifth-growth Bordeaux of Château Battailly – a Pouillac I have always enjoyed.

You can live well at a reasonable price at Belle-Rive.

Château de Larroque

**Château de Larroque
route Toulouse, Gimont,
32200 Gers (on N124, 25km
from Auch, 50km from
Toulouse).
Telephone: (62) 67.77.44.
Rooms E–G;
menus A (weekday lunch), B,
D.
Closed January.
Visa, Amex, Diners.**

I am too old for Toulouse. It is a frenzied, overcrowded city, where everyone seems to be trying to keep up with Concorde and drivers seem to be practising for stock-car racing. Château Larroque may be 50km away but every second of the time takes you closer to peace, quiet, true comfort and beauty.

You reach this elegant nineteenth-century château by a long drive through a well-groomed park of twenty-five acres. Leave your car beside rose-covered stables and walls and climb steps to the graceful front door. Behind is a captivating terrace with lawns, flowers and an abundance of white garden furniture, flanked by trees. A steep drop over the wall leads to woods with thick undergrowth, and beyond, climbing a hill, real farmland with corn growing uphill among copses of old trees. It is rich in birds of many types and colours. There's a lake for fishing and boating, too.

The large drawing room, leading to the terrace, and the library are luxuriously and tastefully furnished, with superb settees and armchairs and most comfortable upright chairs. They have tall windows and doors to the terrace. The dining room is most attractive, with medieval hunting scenes from tapestries. Most bedrooms are enormous and have room for plenty of very comfortable chairs, a table to seat four, rich cloth wall coverings, and thick carpets. Mine had windows to the ceiling overlooking the terrace and the Gascony countryside. The bathroom was large.

The château was built during the Second Empire by a count who was mayor of Gimont and who also gave the town its hospital. He spent too lavishly and went bankrupt. When André Fagedet bought it fifteen years ago it had been left empty for years. All furnishings and fittings had been sold. He has performed miracles in bringing it up to this sumptuous standard, and the atmosphere and welcome are as agreeable as the comfort.

Cheaper than most Châteaux Hotels de France.

A peace lover's retreat from frantic Toulouse.

Auch (24km) – an ancient city straddling the river Gers, it was once capital of Gascony, which is why you can find a statue of the great Gascon Musketeer D'Artagnan there. He is on a landing of the 232-step monumental stairs leading from the river up to Place Salinis and the fourteenth-century Tour d'Armagnac. D'Artagnan was the only one of Alexandre Dumas' Three Musketeers who really lived. Born around 1615 in Château Castelmore near La Tenarèze, as Charles de Batz, he took his mother's aristocratic name d'Artagnan to help him in the Royal Guard and at Court. He carried out secret missions for Louis XIV, was given command of the first company of Musketeers and died at the siege of Maestrich in 1673. His 'Memoirs', fiction by an unknown author, appeared in 1700. Dumas got hold of a copy and based his adventure story on it. The old town of Auch stands on a high spur above the river, dominated by the sixteenth-century pale ochre cathedral with twin bell-towers. Inside are eighteen windows in glorious colour by the sixteenth-century Gascon painter Arnaut de Moles and 113 choir stalls in oak carved with biblical and legendary scenes in the sixteenth century – reminiscent of Amiens cathedral. Lavardens (20km N of Auch) has a castle built in the seventeenth century on the site of an ancient castle of

the Counts of Armagnac. Simorre (S of Auch on D929 to Seissan, left on D129) has a fortified church built in 1304, 'restored' in 1848 by Viollet-le-Duc, with his unhappy trick of altering it.

SW of Gimont (16km), near the hamlet of Cazaux-Savés is the superb Renaissance Château de Caumont. It was built in 1530 by Pierre La Valette, and his grandson, the colourful Duc d'Épernon, was born there. He served Henry III, then Henry IV (the Protestant Henry of Navarre) as Governor of Guyenne, colonel-general of French infantry and Admiral of France. When Henry IV turned Catholic to get the crown, the Duke stayed Protestant. Some say he was an ancestor of mine.

Gimont is a great centre for pâtés and foie gras. Les trois foies gras au naturel were on the dearer menu, so I paid more than I usually do for dinner although I know that the menu at half the price, which changes daily, is very good value. That night it was raw vegetables with a choice of dips, lotte (monkfish) in hazelnut oil and creamed chives, followed by a plate of cooked young vegetables served as a separate course (hurrah!), shoulder of lamb cooked with flowers of thyme, not the usual rosemary, a good salad and a choice from the trolley of superb pâtisseries for which André Fagedet is renowned.

My dearer menu started with crayfish tails in a vividly green and almost over-delicate cream of ciboulette sauce (chives), served with balls of melon.

Next came the three foie gras – goose, duck and chicken – au naturel, sprinkled liberally with pieces of truffle.

The plate of young cooked vegetables followed. Then I chose confit de canard. The duck was cut rather thin but beautifully cooked.

I asked for cheese with my salad and got a fine local ewe cheese. Then a beautiful light cake with fresh strawberries in it. I found the cooking excellent.

The wine list has been very thoughtfully chosen, with two very expensive wines – Château Margaux 1969 and Château d'Yquem – a good choice of medium-priced Bordeaux, Beaujolais and rather dearer Burgundy, and a good

choice of cheaper wines from all around. A meal like this really deserved a Chablis to start and a nice claret to follow, such as 1976 Château Baronne de Rothschild Haut Médoc or the 1975 Château de Roques Saint Emilion. But I like to try regional wines if I can and there were some interesting cheap reds.

This Auch area is really Armagnac brandy country, rivalling Condom. I have tried the sweet white local Pacherence as 'elevenses' but not the dry. It proved to be a typical, rather acidic local plonk, with no finesse, but not unpleasant.

Madarin, the regional red wine, is underestimated. The local Tannat grape, which is mixed with Cabernet, gives it a tannic touch. It is rich flavoured, almost purple in colour, but varies much in taste from one producer to another. The Vignobles Laplace wine on Larroque's list could be mistaken for a Bordeaux. The Domaine Boucasseé has more of the Madarin character.

There are four Côtes de Buzet wines on the list, little known to most Frenchmen outside the South West. They come from half-way between Bordeaux and Auch, are Bordeaux-style, from the two Cabernet grapes and Merlot, and are aged for at least two or three years in oak, making them very fruity. The two best wines are here – Cuvée Napoleon, from the Co-operative of Vignons and Château de Gueyze, both 1979 and just right. Try them – you could be fooled into thinking they *were* clarets.

Cheapest on the list is a Fronton, from north of Toulouse, nearly all drunk in Toulouse. One of the two best is here – Château Bellevue-La-Forêt. It is an AC wine now.

Château de Perigny
86190 Vouillé (Vienne) – just
off N149 Vouillé-Poitiers road
along D43.
Telephone: (49) 51.80.43.
Rooms H;
menus C, D, F.
Visa, Amex, Euro, Diners.

To me this is a heavenly place. It deserves a stay of at least a week. Alas, I have only stayed single nights. Before you fall in love with it, as I have, it is only fair to say something about the cost.

It is a Relais et Châteaux Hotel, and that means one of the best in Europe. Taking the cheapest room, a very nice one, and eating the middle priced menu, dinner, bed and breakfast would cost around £45 each for two of you. Not cheap, but for a hotel like this I think it is a bargain. And many businessmen visiting Poitiers, 17km away, seem to agree. They drive out to stay.

The old stone turreted château, used now as bedrooms with a high season breakfast room, is in a huge park of beautiful woods and meadows in undulating country. It is set apart from the public rooms, so it is very peaceful, and it is a joy to look out on to glorious countryside when you awake.

The other rooms have been converted charmingly from low stone farm buildings and here too are some family apartment-rooms. The bar lounge is cosy and comfortable, with a log fire for winter. The pleasant dining room seems uncluttered. And in summer you can eat under straw shades at tables speckled around a terrace garden among rockeries and flowers. There is an outside summer bar, too, and you can breakfast, take an apéritif or just drink steadily beside a large, heated terrace swimming pool.

The Château has its own riding stables, and as you walk round the estate you meet some of the horses grazing in the meadows. A walk round the fields and woodland paths of the 170-acre estate works up a nice appetite and there are another 7,500 acres of woodland beyond. If that does not give you enough exercise there are three hard tennis courts, hidden behind trees so that the world will not see how rusty you are. And two saunas for recovery. For gentler souls, there is trout fishing in the grounds.

The Brossard family have a

LOCAL DRIVES

Poitiers (17km on N149) is not beautiful but has superb churches. Within the Palais de Justice are a medieval tower from the Dukes of Aquitaine's palace, an historic room (with the three biggest fireplaces in France) Where Joan of Arc was cross examined, and where Richard Lionheart was proclaimed Duke of Anjou. Charles Martel halted the Moorish invasion of Europe at Poitiers in 732. The Black Prince, with the help of our irresistible archers, routed the French before lunch in 1356, taking twice as many prisoners as he had troops. Du Guescelin got it back for France later and Jean, Duke of Berry, kept marauding English bands from their looting by treating them to drinks. Sensible man. In the busy market square is the church of Notre-Dame-la-Grande, famous in France for its decorated façade, twelfth-century Romanesque of Poitevin, now damaged by age.

way of making you feel like a house guest without letting the service slip.

Furnishings are what the French call 'raffiné' – not so much 'refined' as we know it but unostentatious good taste.

Food & Drink

Le Perigny has a fairly cheap changing menu which pleases the *Gault* guide, but in such surroundings I would always be tempted to go for the big menu.

The young chef Dominque Daudon is inventive. Even the salmon is smoked at the hotel, but it costs 25F extra. The speciality among starters is millefeuille de petits gris à la coriandre – tiny snails in flaky pastry. But I prefer the delicately tasty fish terrine with a sort of fresh herb mayonnaise.

For the fish course the sole is braised in Sauvignon wine and served with delicious freshly-made noodles with cream – a succulent dish. But I am a sucker for truly-fresh salmon, and Dominique serves it with a sauce I love – Mirepoix, made by stewing celery, onions, diced carrots in butter with a little thyme and bay leaf (for meat dishes, you add ham). It was invented for a Duke of Lévis-Mirepoix, which sounds like a brand of French jeans.

When it is available, there is only one main dish for me – pintadeau à l'embeurrée de choux et à l'ail – guinea fowl sautéed with butter-boiled cabbage and garlic. There is a lot more to it than that. I believe guinea fowl, like pheasant and especially pigeon, is better tight casseroled than roast or sautéed. You never can tell how tough it will be. But Dominique Daudon has a way of making all guinea fowl tender in a mixture of butter and oil. The cabbage is blanched in quarters then cooked in butter and mashed potato, and served with cooked celery, leek whites, little turnips and twelve cloves of garlic blanched in oil. It is a splendid dish, but not quite in the same class when pigeon replaces the guinea fowl. Then I would go for braised chicken in port wine sauce.

The cheeseboard is satisfactory. The special dessert is tarte tiède aux reinettes acidulées. Fair enough, if you have not had apple tarts lately. The apple tart fashion is spreading from Normandy all over France. Those French apple growers certainly know how to market their products. But a lukewarm apple tart (tiède) – no thank you. 'Tiède' is a Nouvelle fashion, at its worst with salads. Yet the French were the first to complain about lukewarm food in Spain and cold plates in Britain. Ironic.

I would stick to the desserts of the day, and gâteaux, or perhaps the unusual and pleasant sabayon (zabaglione) made with Cointreau.

The food is good, but this is a hotel where the site, the scenery, the atmosphere, and the friendly service are more important.

The wine list is very sensible. I wish more hotels of this standard would stop being quite so snobbish and give a wider choice. Prices are sensible, too, for such a hotel. For an apéritif and with fish, there are perfectly drinkable Sauvignon and Chardonnay whites at fair prices, a fairly good Sancerre, and one of my favourite Muscadets, Château de la Bretesche.

There are also some superb wines – 1977 Château Latour, one of the great premier cru (first growth or 'top') wines of Bordeaux, a very splendid 1972 Château Palmer, a Margaux wine I have not seen in England for years, and a real 1972 Gesweiler Chambertin (not Charmes or Gevrey but

pure Chambertin). Will someone please treat me to a bottle for my birthday?

Down to earth, there's a good 1979 Bourgueil Domaine du Grand Clos to go well with the guinea fowl, and the Rhône white 1979 Crozes Hermitage, would suit the salmon – we don't often see it now in Britain; we have become used to lighter white wines. Salmon does not need anything very dry. A lighter red would be an alternative, 1979 Rully (Domaine de Renarde), for instance. In the Basque country around Bayonne, they cook the wonderful Ardour river salmon in red wine.

French history started at Vouille in 507 AD when Clovis, King of the Franks, defeated and killed the Visigoth King Alaric – uniting the country as far as Bordeaux and Toulouse.

Château de Pray

**Château de Pray
B.P. 146, 37400 Amboise,
Indre-et-Loire (2½km NE of
Amboise along D751, up small
lane on right, signposted; 2km
from A10 motorway sortie
Amboise).
Telephone: (47) 57.23.67.
Rooms E, F;
menus B, C;
half-board F.
Closed 31 December to 10
February.
Visa, Euro, Amex, Diners.**

This enchanting little château is in the best position of the many attractive châteaux or manor houses in the Loire converted into hotels. From a wooded hill it looks down on Amboise, the river and the bank opposite.

I love it. The whole atmosphere is like staying the weekend in a friend's château home.

It was built in the thirteenth-century and the two round towers with pointed roofs still survive from this feudal fortress. One has a bigger circumference than the other. They are joined by a sixteenth-century Renaissance house with a charming terrace, and below its steps are lawns.

Inside is a very pleasant dining room overlooking the terrace, a lounge, a bar, and an attractive staircase leading to bedrooms with period furniture, some in the round towers.

André Farard and his wife are a very sympathetic couple and the service is quietly excellent.

The Loire is once again so popular for tourists that most hotels seem to have been caught up in the modern rush of providing for people with a tight schedule. Château de Pray belongs to the old, more spacious days of travel. The formal garden and the attractive park with old trees cut it off from the world outside. Yet it is a fine centre for seeing other châteaux. Château d'Amboise is down the road, gorgeous Chenonceux 8km away, Chaumont 47km, Azay-le-Rideau 45km, Cheverny 45km, and Blois 35km.

Near Amboise in the forest is a European version of a pagoda. An owner of de Pray, Jean d'Aubigny, built another château here at Chanteloup. It has disappeared, but the Duke de Choiseul, Louis XV's minister bought it and when Madame du Barry became the King's mistress, she had him banished to this estate. Choiseul set up his own 'court', which proved more popular than Versailles, and when his exile from Paris ended, built this pagoda in appreciation of friends who had risked the King's wrath to stay with him. The view from the top is splendid.

The part of Amboise château left after the Revolution is impressive and interesting. Charles VII stole it from the Counts of Amboise. Louis XI gave it to his queen. Their son, later Charles VIII, brought back from Italy, in 1495, Italian artists and craftsmen who changed French artistic styles. Francis I, the flamboyant king, turned it into the centre of court junketings, a sort of earlier Versailles, with festivals, balls, masquerades, tournaments. He brought Leonardo da Vinci here and the great artist finished his life at the nearby Clos Lucé, a fifteenth-century manor where you can see his

bedroom, his drawings and models of machines he invented.

Catherine de Medici, widowed queen, brought her boy-king son, Francis II, and his girl wife Mary, later Queen of Scots, here when Protestants were rising up after the St Bartholomew's Day massacre. In 1560, a misguided Protestant arranged for hundreds to meet him at Amboise to start a revolt. Betrayed to 'Scarface', the evil Duke de Guise, they were tortured, broken, and hanged from castle balconies, still writhing in agony, for days. Royals and Court would come out after dinner to watch them,

like a theatrical show. The royal family met their reward: the boy king Francis II died within months, his brother Charles IX died in terror after a blood-stained reign, Henry III and the Duke of Guise were murdered and Mary Stuart was beheaded.

Food & Drink

Gourmets have castigated Loire chefs for not being inventive. But the Loire is the fruit and vegetable garden of France, produces game from the Orléans forest (venison, partridge, hare), superb pork, lamb from Berry, and duck,

Château de Chenonceaux (8km): the most beautiful house I have ever seen. It was designed by a woman, Katherine Briconnet, between 1513 and 1521 to be lived in, rather than to withstand attack. Another woman, Diane de Poitiers, mistress of Henry II, added a bridge between the château and Cher river banks.

When Henry was killed accidentally in a jousting match, his wife Catherine de Medici took Chenonceaux and gave Diane the draughty pile of Chaumont, which she soon left. Catherine had the splendid two-storey gallery built on the bridge and laid out the park. She held extraordinary parties with mermaids, nymphs, satyrs and cavaliers welcoming guests. There are splendid stories of love affairs, intrigues and politics in the history of this magnificent château. (Open daily; son et lumière shows late evening mid-June to mid-September.)

Also see Château Chambord (47km), Beauregard and Cheverny (both on D765 from Blois): see entry under L'Escale du Port Arthur, St-Hilaire-St-Mesmin, page 72.

wild and tame, from Touraine, where Château de Pray is situated, pike, eels, perch, salmon and trout from the rivers, chicken from everywhere, and wonderful fruit (apricots, peaches, pears, quinces, plums from which the famous Tours prunes are made, and dessert grapes). So most people are happy with these delicious fresh ingredients, freshly cooked in classical dishes and with a multitude of pâtés, sausages and cheeses. Asparagus is lovely and fairly cheap in spring, sweet, tender broad beans are served in early summer and lovely mushrooms and other fungi in autumn.

Cooking at the Château de Pray is mainly straightforward and excellent. The menus are good value. One Sunday lunch recently I had not booked, and nor had a family who followed me in, but we were found tables by a little judicious juggling, and I had an excellent meal. First there was raw beef dried in the sun, then a chicken mousse pâté, light and very delicate flavour. I had a simply delicious salmon-trout for the fish course, followed by roast lamb with three vegetables. From the cheeseboard I chose the best known local Touraine cheese, Saint-Maure, a creamy goat's milk, and a Pithiviers cow's milk cheese from around Orléans.

The Château de Pray is known far and wide for its pâtisseries and a glance at the trolley will tell you why. I had a simple strawberry tart – simply perfect.

To show how straightforward the cooking is, the specialities on the card are poached salmon with beurre blanc (the Touraine favourite sauce of shallots cooked in white wine and whipped up with butter), braised duck with olives, noisette de porc au pruneaux (fillet of pork in a cream sauce with the local prunes) and pâtisseries.

Loire white wines are well represented on the list here, of course (Sancerre, Pouilly Fumé, Muscadet, Saumur, Vouvray). The house wine is the local Montlouis, a dryish *pétillant* (still slightly sparkling) white wine compared unfavourably sometimes with Vouvray from directly across the Loire – and cheaper.

Saumur wines are far better known in France than Britain, where we think almost entirely of the sparkling Saumur. Ackerman of Saumur were the first to make a sparkling wine by the Champagne method outside Champagne, back in 1811, and I have still not tasted a better sparkler from outside Champagne. But there are some good still wines from there, too. There is a Saumur Champigny red on the de Pray list at a lowish price and it is worth trying. Lighter than Bourgueil or Chinon – good with salmon. It was fashionable in France about ten years ago. Now heavy, strong Cahors is fashionable and there is one of the very best on this list – Comte de Monpézat.

The speciality red of de Pray is St Nicholas de Bourgueil, another heavy, dark, strong wine with a fruity smell and strong taste which goes splendidly with game, duck, goose and beef dishes, and for me is just made for drinking on a winter's night in Britain with a real old English steak and kidney pudding.

Domaine de la Tortinière

Domaine de la Tortinière
Les Gués de Veigné, 37250
Montbazon, Indre-et-Loire
(1.5km N of Montbazon, just
off N10 on D287).
Telephone: (47) 26.00.19.
Rooms F–H, apartments H;
meals D–E;
half-board F–H.
Closed 16 November to 1
March.
Visa, Euro.

I just cannot think that I am staying in a hotel when I am visiting this Second Empire turreted château in a superb park. I feel that I am a guest of Denise Olivereau-Capron in her family home.

It is her family home. She lived here with her father and mother from 1954 and made it into a hotel after her father's death. She and her three children live in one of the buildings, and her staff, too, treat you as a guest. White with a grey roof, this handsome house stands on a hill with 100 acres of woodland, meadows, flowerbeds and lawns running down to the Indre river. A manor house has stood here since 1562, but no one knows who planted the rare trees, which include cedars of Lebanon and two three-headed sophoras. And in autumn wild cyclamen adds a colourful carpet to the ceiling of autumn leaves.

All the bedrooms are individual, comfortable, and pretty or interesting. You might sleep in one of the round towers, in a cosy, charming room in the old stable block, or an apartment in one of the three *pavillons* a few steps away from the main house. Or you could have the space-age room – a very modern room in white with a big round white bed and a TV set up in the ceiling. 'What a splendid room for a tempestuous love affair,' I said. 'All our rooms are splendid for lovers,' smiled Denise.

This is a *Relais du Silence* so you cannot go wrong here if you want '*calme, tranquilité, repos*'. There is a swimming pool, and fishing and boating on the river.

I love it. So near the busy N10, so handy for the Loire, its resorts and châteaux, yet a million miles from traffic and people.

A château cookery course held here in March and April, including dinners with neighbouring owners. A wonderful souvenir of France but very pricey indeed.

Azay-le-Rideau (20km on D17) a pleasant old town, its elegant Gothic Château d'Azay, almost as lovely as Chenonceaux. Partly built on piles in the river bed and surrounded by water, the château's 'fortifications' are mere décor. It was just a beautiful house. Francis I's financial minister built it. Now it is a superb museum of Renaissance furniture and tapestries. There are guided tours of the château almost every day. The gardens are freely open to the public, with son et lumière on various days, and 1 June to 24 August inclusive.

On route from Montbazon you pass near to Saché, the sixteenth-century château which the writer de Balzac adored. There is a Balzac museum.

Tours (13km north) – now heavily industrialized, crowded and disappointing (rue Colbert in the old town is a good shopping street for food). Magnificent châteaux within range of Tortinière include: Chinon (41km); Montrichard – ruins of medieval castle where Philippe Auguste of France besieged Richard Lionheart (40km); Château de Gué Pean at Monthou-sur-Cher – magnificent Renaissance château in white with a blue roof (9km from Montrichard); Chenonceaux, the most beautiful house in the world (31km); Amboise – partly ruined but impressive and with an interesting history (39km); and Chaumont (60km).

Food & Drink

From the cosy lounge, you go downstairs to a bright dining room with garden décor and views across the valley. Indeed, it must have been a garden room.

Young François Hervoil is an inventive chef who deserves higher recognition in France. He believes in serving vegetables, thank goodness, which seem to be taboo in many restaurants except as plate decorations. Mind you, he does not serve them in the quantities of classical French cooking of old. Everything is produced in the kitchen, from duck foie gras to the smoked salmon. Of his interesting starters, I like best his smoked salmon with salmon marinaded in fresh lime juice and green pepper, served on a mixed salad. I was also pleased with his salaison de canard – thin slices of confit of duck, dried duck breasts and gizzard on a green salad. You have no need to worry about translating his unusual dishes – the card has an English version alongside the French. I wish that some London restaurants would do me the same courtesy.

I had recently a beautiful braised sandre, the delicately flavoured Loire river fish, served with a white butter sauce. I like, too, the little fillets of fresh salmon and sandre twined, braised, with basil butter sauce.

Dodine de pigeonneau de Touraine is one of the best pigeon dishes I have tasted. A young pigeon is boned, stuffed with chicken and morels (a sort of mushroom) and roasted. The duck magret is cooked in the old way with a creamy orange sauce, and served with sweet and savoury vegetables. But my favourite is saddle of lamb with a mildly garlic creamy sauce and curry flavoured onion purée. The lamb's flavour is really enhanced.

Cheeses are served with home-made walnut bread. Desserts are delicious and I do not know which to pick. My own favourite is a strawberry crêpe, with the strawberries poached then rolled in a thin pancake and served with raspberry custard. The chef's speciality is gratin de framboises aux amandes – a gorgeous confection of whipped cream mixed with whipped confectioner's custard and raspberry liqueur. The raspberries are put on top of this mixture, chopped roasted almonds are added, then more of the mixture, icing sugar put on top, and the dish glazed under a grill. It is served hot.

The wine list is well chosen, with sensible prices by current restaurant standards, including for Bordeaux. More than half the wines are from the Loire valley.

Loire wines, coming from the far north of the wine world, vary so much from year to year with climate that they seem different wines. The one Muscadet on the list here is outstanding – a 1982 'sur lie' from Métaireau. 'Sur lie' means that the wine is left on the lees until bottling, and some experts say that it makes little difference. But with a good wine I think it makes all the difference, giving a fruitier flavour. Two interesting whites not many people know are from Anjou. The Savennières is from La Coulée de Serrant, a tiny vineyard producing the best wine of this area. But Savennières whites are made with the Chenin grape (also called Pineau de Loire) and need keeping a few years. Young Chenin wines taste acid and sometimes even sulphury. The other is a 1978 Quart de Chaume, from the Layon river – a subtle wine tasting almost perfumed. A dry and a sweet Vouvray are from Marc Brédif of Rochecorbon, probably the greatest Vouvray blender.

There are several tempting red wines, but I would not look past the 1976 Bourgueil les Marquises or for a bargain wine St Nicolas de Bourgueil La Chevallerie, both from Audebert, one of the very top producers. Bourgueil wines have a definite character, with a touch of tannin taste, a good bouquet which some liken to raspberries, and are very good value.

If François Hervoil's excellent meals can be a bit pricey, the wines keep the balance.

L'Escale du Port Arthur
205 rue de l'Eglise, St-Hilaire-
St-Mesmin, 45580 Loiret
(15km from Orléans).
Telephone: (38) 76.30.36.
Rooms A–B;
menus A, B;
half-board C, two sharing.
Closed 1 to 22 November;
Mondays in winter.
Visa.

Renoir would surely have painted the terrace of this hotel right on the bank of the little Loiret river. On a fine day you can sit under umbrellas with an aperitif bottle of Loire blanc de blancs on the white table and become mesmerized into delightful dreams by the fast-flowing river and the gentle movement and sound of the lime trees, big willows and tall birches capped with crows' nests.

Swallows dive and weave over the water, ducks hug the banks seeking worms, wavelets slap against the flat-bottomed boats slowly twisting on their ropes by the river bank.

In inclement weather, you can drink or eat in the glass-enclosed addition to the dining room, still with only the terrace and an old towpath between you and the river, and an open fire across the room to warm you.

It is not a pretty hotel, but it is a place of true quiet and calm, a world apart from the big Loire river, into which the Loiret flows, with its nuclear power station, gravel pits, big camp

sites, and beaches with frîtes vans and snack bars.

You choose this hotel for its tranquillity and its excellent value. The service is good, but some rooms are fairly basic – simple furniture, velvet bedspreads and curtains, but no carpet. But you may well get a view of the river.

Food & Drink

Jacques Reichlin is my sort of chef. He likes strong flavours. He has subtle touches, too, like his beautifully-blended salad dressings, but even the compulsory magret de canard (duck's breasts) is served with peppers. Some of his specialities are a joy.

Even the cheapest menu has not only a choice in each course but four courses – salad or cheese of your choice, followed by a choice of desserts. The slightly dearer menu has four courses, too, and often includes my two favourites of this hotel.

The first is salade de crottin roti. If you do not know what

The floral park of Orleans (86 acres) has massed blooms from April to November, tulips, iris, dahlias, chrysanthemums, a quarter of a million rose bushes, among old trees, fountains and modern sculptures. Cultivation is greatly helped by the waters of the Loiret which bubble out here at a temperature of 12–15°C/54–59°F. Its true source is at St Benoît, but it re-emerges here. In winter many ducks, geese and even flamingoes take up residence. A little train runs through the park.

West along the Loire and over to the north bank is Meung, a nice little town with walks under limes along the river Mauves, a Loire tributary loved by fishermen. The old bishop's castle (open Easter to November) is still beautifully furnished. In the last days of the Hundred Years War it was the headquarters of General Talbot, who lost to Joan of Arc after winning forty fights, and of the Earl of Salisbury, who had his head blown off at the Siege of Orléans.

There is an embarrassment of châteaux along the south bank of the Loire. Chambord is the most spectacular. Its park, surrounded by walls twenty miles long, is gorgeous and still rich in deer and wild boar. Its house is splendid from outside, but not comfortable within. It has 440 rooms, separated by 80 staircases, and 365 chimneys. It was built for hunting by the outrageous and amusingly

ostentatious Francis I, said to be always hunting stags or women, who was determined to outshine his rivals Henry VIII and Emperor Charles V. He used it for only forty days. The whole court went with him and 12,000 horses carried their servants, furniture, crockery and baggage. (Closed Tuesdays; son et lumière from 1 May to 30 September).

Beauregard Château, also built for Francis I as a hunting lodge, is smaller and prettier. A gallery has 363 portraits of famous people and a Delft-tiled floor showing Louis XIII's army. It is still lived in. So is the pleasant seventeenth-

century Château de Cheverney nearby – by the Marquis of Vibray, descendant of the original owner. It has lavish decorations and seventeenth-century furnishings, a fine park, and an excellent pack of hounds. But to me the most beautiful is Chenonceux, south of Amboise (see Hotel Château du Pray, Amboise, page 66).

I chose it for its charming position and as a centre for exploring the Loire and its châteaux

crottin means, perhaps I should not tell you. But I shall. It means goat's manure – this goat's cheese is supposed to smell like it. It does certainly smell strong – but so do other cheeses. It has a lovely flavour, particularly when grilled and served hot. In this salad, two rounds are served on thin slices of toast from baguette loaves – the long sticks. They are surrounded by a salad of chopped lettuce, curly endive ('frisée') and tomato in a perfectly balanced mixture of wine vinegar and walnut oil, and sprinkled liberally with quarters of fresh walnuts. Gorgeous!

The other dish is slightly seasonal – filet de saumon 'sauvage' (wild, not farmed salmon) aux graines de moutarde.

Simply, a good slice of salmon in a subtle but flavoursome sauce flavoured with grain mustard, coarse-ground so that there are little lumps in it, which is popular in France.

There are some tempting alternatives. A super starter is fricassée de St-Jacques aux cèpes – chopped fried scallops with cèpes, the most delightful and soft-flavoured of a multitude of fungi which the French eat. And I had a splendid local dish of Orléans – coquelet Solognote – stuffed chicken cooked in onion and tomato sauce.

Although there is a good Sancerre Thomas white wine at a fair price here is a chance to try a once-famous wine which is now little known to Britons – Quincy. Classed as a Loire wine, it comes really from the Cher river area. It is made from Sauvignon grapes, is crisp, fruity and slightly flinty, like a Pouilly Fumé. It was one of the first wines in France to get an appellation contrôlée label (AC), and has now the second oldest AC rating. This one, from Raymond Pipet, is one of the best, and very good value.

The patron, Jean Marquet, has a well-chosen cellar of red wines, strong in cheaper local wines including a Touraine Gamay from Girard. The Gamay grape is used for Beaujolais, but this wine is a bit more acid. The 1981 Château Gaillard from Touraine-Mesland on the right bank of the Loire is cheap and very good value, and I thought it went well with the salmon. So, I should think, would the 1980 Château Dintrains, a première Côtes de Bordeaux – excellent value.

Logis de Beaulieu

Le Logis de Beaulieu and
Restaurant L'Alambic
Saint Laurent de Cognac,
16100 Cognac, Charente.
Telephone: (45) 82.30.50.
Rooms B–G;
menus B, C, D;
breakfast A;
half-pension E–G.
Closed 16 December to 1
January.
Visa, Amex, Diners.

A brandy baron from nearby
Cognac built Beaulieu in a
small park in 1918 and it might
have strayed from 1920s
Somerset. It is known now for
its choice of 105 cognac brand-
ies, openly displayed for your
temptation.

You come on it suddenly
along lanes among vineyards
between the A10 Paris-
Bordeaux motorway and the
old N10. Turn south on the
N141 Cognac–Saintes road, not
north at St Laurent, cross the
Charente river and take D732
towards Pons. You can leave
the A10 at Pons (13km) or Saintes (18km), the N10 at Angoulême.

The twenty-one bedrooms are
mostly big enough for Danielle
Biancheri to furnish them with
fin de siècle pieces, which
make me feel secure and comfortable.

Madame Biancheri arranges
boat trips along the Charente
river, which meanders through
lush prés – meadows flooded
in winter, dotted in summer
with cows which produce superb Charente cream and butter. Boats run from Cognac and

Saintes from Whitsun to mid-
September.

She also arranges visits to
leading brandy houses and
chais, where brandy matures
in casks, and is blended and
bottled. The world's largest re-
serves of old brandy are at the
house of Hennessy, where you
can see a film of brandy production and a museum with
old instruments and barrels.

Brandy was invented in the
Renaissance when the Dutch
objected to shipping costs for
inferior local wine. To reduce
weight, they had it distilled
and called it Brandewijn (burnt
wine) – Instant Wine, just add
water!

Microscopic mushrooms
thriving on alcoholic fumes
have turned the buildings in
Cognac browny-black. Before
modern ventilation, men
working in the chais got drunk
breathing the fumes.

There's Otard brandy maturing in the cellars of what is left
of Château de Valois, home of
Francis I and later prison for
Britons taken in Canada in the
Seven Years War. Their grafitti
is still there.

Food & Drink

Georges Biancheri, chef of Beaulieu's 'L'Alambic' restaurant and winner of a Grand Cordon d'Or Français, warns you on his *carte* – *La cuisine est faite au moment*. While you are waiting he suggests you try an aperitif – Pineau – young Charente white or rosé wine with brandy, invented by an absent-minded local pouring new wine into a barrel of cognac.

Charente's chefs don't need frills. Some of France's richest land gives them superb butter, fine beef, salt-grazed (*pré-salé*) lamb from south of La Rochelle, lovely vegetables and fruit, including Charentais melons. Fish, too – oysters from Marennes, mussels from the farms of Boyardville off the isle of Oléron, lampreys (eels) from estuaries, trout and anguilles (more eels) from rivers, and pork from around Angoulême. Cooking is based on butter, laced with cream and wine. Most is what the French call 'honest and direct'. Georges' cuisine is more imaginative than most.

His five-course mid-price menu is usually outstanding value and changes constantly with seasons and market. I would certainly look at it first.

From the card, I would choose a technically unbalanced meal, with two sorts of shellfish, starting with Arvert oysters, fresh each day in season. Then mouclade à la Rochelaise, the gourmet's moules marinières – mussels cooked in a sauce of shallots, wine, parsley, butter, with thick cream, pineau and a touch of curry powder.

To avoid two shellfish courses, replace mouclade with his local trout braised in Muscadet, in a velouté sauce made with crème fraîche (slightly soured cream).

Charantais lamb is good, but I would not miss Georges' fricassée de veau au vinaigre de Xères (tender veal liver, sautéed, then cooked in a cream sauce with wine vinegar mixed with sherry).

The cheeseboard is a delight. I like Piguille, a creamy white curd cheese of cow's milk (it

LOCAL DRIVES Jarnac, by the river on the N141 east from Cognac, is known for its brandy market, Château Courvoisier, and a notorious duel fought in 1547 between Gui Chabot, Lord of Jarnac, and La Chataigneriae, friend of France's Henry II. In front of the King, Queen (Catherine of Medici) and the King's mistress Diane de Poitiers, Chabot, who was losing, cadishly thrust his sword through his rival's hamstring. A stab in the back in France is still called un coup de Jarnac. D22 on the right after Jarnac follows the river to historic Abbaye de Bassac. Further on, attractive little roads D7 and D72 lead to Angoulême – industrial but pleasant, perched on a rocky spur with ramparts turned into walks with views over the Charente Valley. At Promenade Beaulieu is a plaque to General Resnier who, in 1806, aged seventy-eight, took off in a wing-flapping machine he had invented for Napoleon's troops to invade England. He fell in the river, but only broke an arm.

To Saintes from the Logis use D84 along the river's north bank, a sinuous but rewarding run to Chantiers. Turn left at La Baine (1km) to a pretty river site with two islands.

Saintes' twelfth-century Abbaye aux Dames was one of 500 Romanesque churches built in the Middle Ages with gifts from pilgrims staying overnight at Saintes on route from Paris to the tomb of St James of Compostella in Spain – a journey nicely combining religious fervour and tourism. The abbey was used for educating girls of noble families. Mme de Montespan, Louis XIV's mistress, was an Old Girl. Old Saintes has a maze of tiny medieval streets down to the river and an avenue promenade of eighteenth-century houses.

Pons has lovely buildings, from a hilltop down to the river Seugne. The Renaissance Château d'Oussous (1km SE) was moved stone-by-stone last century from near Cognac – à l'Américaine.

You can enjoy travel's rarest gift - seclusion - in the 15 acre park and gardens.

can be made of sheep's or goat's milk) and a triangular goat's milk cheese of Aunis, not so strong as Mothe.

In season, local strawberries in local honey make a delicious dessert. Otherwise I like sabayon au pineau – zabaglione of egg yolks with pineau replacing wine. His special sweet is mendicants: of hazlenuts, figs, almonds and raisins (representing the four colours of the mendicant friars) soused in cognac (like the friars, perhaps!).

A first glance at the Beaulieu's wine list inspires awe. 1949 St Emilion Château Saint-Georges, 1967 Château Lafitte-Rothschild; 1948 Hospices de Beaune. Peasants like me can take heart – there are also a local Champerle Charente white (slightly tart), a Côtes du Rhône red and a good value Provence rosé at very low prices.

With oysters, pick a sharpish Gros Plant (very cheap) or much better value Epinay Muscadet. Sancerre is overpriced, as nearly everywhere.

Choose an ordinary red with mouclade to suit the liver and cheese, too. Loire Bourgueil is dark and flavoursome; 1975 Château Lalande, not great but most palatable, is the best bargain among the red Bordeaux. Among a string of splendid wines the Bordeaux seem better value than the Burgundies. Beaulieu has a great wine cellar.

Twenty-seven Champagnes are mostly mouthwatering vintage wines at over 200F a bottle.

Paradise from a brandy bottle costs an awful lot a glass if from Briand, a little less if from Hennessy. Like the word 'Napoleon', 'Paradis' is not a standard grade or age but is in the eye of the bottler and palate of the drinker. Nor is VSOP a grade, though it usually means an older, liqueur quality brandy, not a younger three-star. Fine means a blend from Grande or Petite Champagne districts. Districts are official. In order of importance they are Grande Champagne, Petite Champagne, Borderies, Fins Bois, Bons Bois and Bois Ordinaires (which goes right out to La Rochelle and the isles of Oléron and Ré).

The Logis' 105 different cognacs are all old, from Bisquit VSOP at 20F a glass to Paradis at about 7 times as much.

Moulin de Montalétang

Moulin de Montalétang
St Moreil, 23400 Bourganeuf,
Creuse (13km SE of
Bourganeuf on D941 and D22;
40km from Limoges).
Telephone: (55) 54.92.72.
Rooms B–D;
menus A, C.
Closed 1 November to 15
March.
Restaurant closed
Wednesdays in low season.
Visa.

The Moulin changed hands in
the winter of 1984–85 and
alterations are expected before
it reopens in the spring.

Just a family-run two-star country inn with good food. But
what an idyllic situation. In
lovely wild, hilly and wooded
country, with near-primitive
hamlets, it is a converted
water-mill in a 350-acre estate
with four shallow lakes – *étangs*
– rich in trout and covering
forty acres.

There are some lovely walks
around here, but don't get lost,
either walking or driving. It is
not exactly in St Moreil itself,
so keep your eyes open for the
signposts leading to it.

Your reward for finding it is
true peace and relaxation in
what a French guide called 'a
green paradise'. You can fish
for trout free, walk the wood-
lands, take a boat or pedalo on
the lakes, swim, ride a horse,
just sit on the lawns of the
pleasant garden and read, or
look across the river at the
sheep and lambs and the men
working in the orchards, or
lean on the little bridge and
watch the little river hurrying
below. It is a place where you
truly forget what day it is – a
Relais du Silence, promising
'quiet, peace, rest'.

It is run by a young couple
and brother-in-law, who cooks.
They are very friendly and
helpful and overcome a certain
inexperience by hard work.
There is an English-style bar
where fishing stories are told,
and a dining room with such
appalling décor that you wonder who could have done it,
but a lovely garden made and
kept by the patron, Jean-Luc
Delias.

The bedrooms vary a bit.
Some are pretty, others very
ordinary. Mine was pleasant –
a delicate flowery wallpaper
with Pompadour pictures and
a little modern bathroom. But it
is a place for staying outdoors
and enjoying the natural
beauty.

Food & Drink

The chef, M. Simon, brother-
in-law of the patron, has some
really delightful dishes in good
value menus. In the cheaper
menu I had a very good fish
terrine served hot, and in the
dearer menu a delightful dish
of river fish in flaky pastry with

superb sauce. His sauces are generally very good and varied – traditional thick sauces with heavier dishes, a delicious watercress sauce, à la Nouvelle, with the breasts of chicken.

His own speciality is lapereau (young rabbit) à la gelée de Sauvignon, but I do not like rabbit enough to choose it. My favourite of his dishes is salmis de pintadeau – a really rich and winey dish of guinea fowl. First the bird is half-roasted, then sautéed in wine to finish it. He served plenty of vegetables, too, plus frîtes.

It is fashionable to decry frîtes but most French people still like them with most dishes, and properly cooked they are one of the world's greatest vegetables.

He serves very good desserts, including delicious cerise jubilé – cherries poached, then flambéed with kirsch, a cherry spirit, and an interesting soufflé with pistachio nuts.

There are some good local cheeses, mostly cow. But if you like Roquefort try the Limousin slightly milder equivalent, Bleu de Basillac, a sheep's cheese, of course.

The hotel has a good strong list of Bordeaux wines, but frankly I think it is a bit too strong on expensive wines. I like the cooking very much but I don't think it rates a Lafite-Rothschild with it! It must be very difficult in France when so little wine is produced in your area, and I did have a St Nicolas de Bourgueil at a near-bargain price, and a good Muscadet.

The French have a word for this country side – 'sauvage'

river valley to St Léonard de Noblat, perched on a hill above the valleys of three rivers. The church has a spectacular square belfry with a pointed spire, and there are old houses dating back to the thirteenth century.

Limoges (40km) – the city of enamel and porcelain. Enamel work, made from glass with a lead base, started with the monks of St Martial Abbey around the tenth-century, copying the Byzantines who had practised the art since the sixth century. The impressionist painter Renoir worked here as an enamel painter. To see how it is done, go to one of the workshops around place Wilson and rue des Tanneries. Some allow visits during working hours and the window displays are splendid. Porcelain came later to Limoges – in 1771, under the patronage of the Count of Artois. Then kaolin of great purity was found in the region in 1788 – as good as the white clay used in china. The industry grew quickly after the Napoleonic wars and Limoges now makes more than half of France's porcelain.

The municipal museum of Limoges has magnificent enamels dating from the twelfth century, plus two Renoir paintings. The Adrien Dubuché National Museum has 10,000 pieces of porcelain covering the evolution of china through the centuries from all over the world. It is a delight.

LOCAL DRIVES Bourganeuf (13km) – Zizim Tower was part of the former castle of the Knights of St John. A Mohammedan prince, Zizim, tried to steal his brother's throne. Failing this, he sought refuge with Pierre d'Aubusson, the Grand Master of the Order, who commanded the defence of Malta. The prince was 'imprisoned' here in 1493, continuing to live in his accustomed luxury. There are tours from mid-April to mid-September. Tapestries in the town hall include a splendid eighteenth-century Aubusson.

Lac de Vassivière (get on to D5 near St Moreil, turn left to Peyrat, then D13, on to D222, 25km) – man-made lake with inlets and bays; drive right round it. The Touring Club de France has a sailing centre and people can swim, sail, canoe, use a motor boat or hire a pedalo. A national regatta is held over Whitsun. There are restaurants (the best is La Caravelle, with terrace on the lakeshore). The lake has a nice setting of woods and hills. It covers 2,500 acres and was made by damming the river Maulde, a tributary of the Vienne; there are several dams within less than 50km. You can drive back through the

Hostellerie Moulin du Roc

Moulin du Roc
Champagnac-de-Belair, 24530
Dordogne (6km from
Brantôme on D78, D83).
Telephone: (53) 54.80.36.
Rooms G–H;
menus B, D, E.
Closed mid-November to mid-
December; mid-January to
mid-March; restaurant closed
Tuesdays, Wednesdays
midday except for residents.
Visa, Amex, Euro, Diners.

Truly idyllic. Lucien and Solange Gardillou have made a little masterpiece from an old nut-oil mill, and Solange still performs miracles in the kitchen. The place to take a lover, renew a slightly-fading marriage or have a second honeymoon.

Hidden in the wilds, but only 6km from the old town of Brantôme now so popular with tourists, the seventeenth-century mill stands beside a little stream in lovely flower gardens with little wooden bridges. The old machinery is still there, outside and in the little lounge, where you sit around it. The intimate dining room and the beamed salon are exquisitely furnished in antiques and dotted with ornaments. The bedrooms are lavishly furnished with magnificent old pieces, such as huge carved oak four-posters with coiled posts, big old carved chests and wardrobes, old carved oak doors and, in some, great big oil paintings in gilt frames. Some guests find it all a bit overpowering, but I don't. But I suppose that I am some-

thing of a Regency and Louis XV man.

Sitting in the garden eating breakfast amid the vividly-coloured flowers on a summer's morning, from a little table covered with immaculate white linen, laid with fresh-squeezed orange juice, rolls baked fresh each day by Solange Gardillou from fresh-ground flour, jam made by her, and strawberries from the garden, is my idea of how to start a day. Sitting at a table laid with perfect linen, silver cutlery and candlestick, cut crystal glasses, and a bowl of flowers, by the dining room French windows opening on to the garden, with champagne cooling in a tall copper ice bucket beside you, is a good way to start an evening. In the day you can punt yourself along the river, fish for trout, play tennis or go swimming 200 metres away, or ride a horse from nearby stables. It is a great life at the mill.

20,000 bottles of Bordeaux in the wine cellar here!

Brantôme (6km) – medieval and Renaissance town built on an island between two arms of the river Dronne, has suffered recently from too many tourists, so try to see it off-season. André Maurois, who lived nearby, called it 'the most ravishing, the most fairy-like of all the small towns of Périgord'. There are still beautiful buildings, riverside houses with flowered gardens, charming bridges, and the monk's garden of the old abbey said to have been built by Charlemagne in 769, sacked by the Normans who rowed up the river in 849, then rebuilt in the eleventh-century. In a cave behind is a remarkable sixteenth-century bas-relief of the Crucifixion. In the garden is a bust of the sixteenth-century abbot, diplomat, and witty cynical chronicler of court life, known as 'Brantôme' (Pierre de Bourdeilles). Charming riverside walks. Good Tuesday market.

Bourdeilles castle (7km from Brantôme on D18): magnificently built on a rock above the river Dronne, the town on both banks and a medieval mill shaped like a boat. Two castles – a medieval ruin over which the English and French squabbled for centuries, and a Renaissance castle with sumptuous furnishings and decorations, especially the gold room with wall paintings, tapestries and French ceiling. Most furniture is Spanish or Italian. 'Brantôme' was born here. (Open daily except from mid-December to 1 February; Tuesdays in winter.)

Food & Drink

Solange Gardillou has two stars from *Michelin*, two 'to-ques' from the *Gault Millau* guide and many worshipping gastronomes. She combines classical with traditional Péri-gourdine cooking from old recipes she has researched, touched by her own special flair, and I believe that she is one of the greatest cooks of regional dishes in France.

Her three-course cheapish menu is just right for lunch. I like the salad 'Paysanne' (with raw vegetables, such as carrots and onion) with bacon, Roquefort cheese and walnuts. I would choose the middle-priced menu most times, but there are some gorgeous dishes on the card: home-smoked trout, trout from the river stuffed with the subtle fungi cèpes, guinea fowl (pintade) legs stuffed with seed mustard and pasta, lobster salad with wal-nut oil, and the inevitable foie gras dishes.

On the middle menu last time there was a spring salad with a fillet of guinea fowl, cèpes and smoked goose. Next course was trout with a slightly-garlicky parsley sauce. Then a choice of haunch of pintadeau superbly cooked with herbs and pasta or, my own choice, confit de jeune canard. I love potted duck, and this confit with duckling is exceptionally good, with less fat and more flavour than most. Cheeses were carefully chosen, fresh and local, and included the fairly rare ewe's milk cheese of Rocamadour.

La caravanne de desserts is an exceptionally pretty trolley laden with pretty, luscious and tempting confections, many using fresh local fruit. A 'soupe' of fresh fruit is served 'à la Badianne', which is a strong anis (aniseed) spirit – not my bowl of soupe, but Barbara would like it.

Lucien Gardillou's excellent wine list has some superb Bordeaux at very fair prices for such wine. Solange's cooking deserves a bottle. But this is the Dordogne and he has cheaper local wines, too, including a very drinkable Bergerac and a fairly good Pécharmant. Pécharmant is the best of Bergerac reds – rather like a light, lesser St Emilion. Château de Tiregand and Clos de la Montalbanie are good ones.

Don't forget Monbazillac – a golden sweet wine which once rivalled Sauternes. Château de Monbazillac, run by a cooperative now, is still reliable. It goes well enough with dessert. But I like it iced as an 11.30a.m. pre-aperitif. A Mayor of Sauternes taught me that habit. He gave me Château d'Yquem.

le coq arlequin

Hôtel de Paris et du Coq Arlequin
1 boulevard du Dr Roux,
46400 Saint-Céré, Lot (54km SE of Brive; 76km NE of Cahors).
Telephone: (65) 38.02.13.
Rooms with breakfast C–E; menus A, B, C, D; half-board D, E.
Closed January, February and Mondays low-season.

In a corner of this hotel's dining room is a vivid, amusing and brilliant tapestry of a puffed-up cock in a coat of many colours. Le Coq Arlequin – the original masterpiece by Jean Lurçat, friend of Bracque, Picasso and the rest, who turned his genius to reviving the great art of tapestries and ceramics. Look from the front terrace of this hotel to the top of the hill above St-Céré and you will see the sixth-century castle of Saint-Laurent. Here Lurçat lived and worked from 1945 until his death in 1966.

He was a close friend of Gérard Bizat, whose family have owned the hotel for five generations. It was called Hotel de Paris when I first knew it thirty-five years ago. Round the walls of the public rooms are more works by Lurçat and many other artists, including Gérard Bizat himself. He was a career artist until he came back to the hotel to help his father.

It is an intimate, agreeable and gentle hotel which you grow very quickly to love. There is no plan to its buildings or furniture. It has all hap-pened over generations, with some rooms furnished in Empire style, some like an expensive modern apartment in Paris. Another building across an alleyway has been added to the hotel and there an open and a covered terrace have been beautifully furnished with garden furniture. Bedrooms are charming. Service is good and pleasant.

The hotel has a little shop selling specialities of Quercy and the Dordogne, especially truffled foie gras and pâtés and confit of duck and goose, some of it made in the hotel kitchen by the chef, Janine and Gérard Bizat's son, Eric.

St-Céré is a captivating, smiling little town on a tributary of the Dordogne, the river Bave, which runs alongside its main square and some of its lovely houses which date back to the fifteenth to seventeenth centuries. In the casino, around the bar and in an adjoining room, is a permanent exhibition of Jean Lurçat's work. Some of the ceramics are for sale. It is a good way to enjoy his superb richly-

Coming shortly — a swimming pool, barbecue grill and a leisure park.

So many places to see that you will need a week. But here is a circuit to include many of them: Take D673 to Château de Montal (3km) – a remarkable phoenix castle. It was built in 1534 by Jeanne de Balsac for a son who was away at the wars. She hired the greatest builders and artists. Only his body returned. His grief-stricken mother had her window blocked up. In 1879 an asset-stripper auctioned its treasures and sold some of its stone for building in Paris. In 1908 a new owner had it repaired and bought back the treasures from museums and collectors at ransom prices. One stone doorway was missing, so Rodin, the great sculptor, made a new one.

Continue on D673 to Grotte de Presque (caves pillared with slim and thick stalagmites up to 30 feet (9 metres) high, in strangely varying shapes) and then Gouffre de Padirac, a chasm made by the Devil's heel. St Martin accepted his challenge to jump it (all 325 feet (100 metres) on a mule. The mule should have been canonized, too. A refuge shelter in the Hundred Years War and Wars of Religion, it was neglected until 1890. By lift and stairs, you descend 338 feet (103 metres) to a chamber, walk to an underground river and take a boat over strangely trans-lucent waters for half a mile to visit more chambers on foot.

Drive through Alvignac to Rocamadour, one of Europe's most amazing scenes. A

medieval city clamped on a 500 foot (152 metre) rock face; magnificent despite too many tourists shops and tourists. See it from the road terrace at L'Hospitalet, preferably at night or in the morning sun. From the castle at the top the town works its way down through a maze of old houses, towers, rocks and oratories to a road still high above a river valley. Founded by St Amadour, a recluse. Pilgrims used to climb 216 steps on their knees and in chains. Back to Alvignac and along D20 to Carennac, a gorgeous village on the Dordogne river. D30, then left on D4 to Castelnau, with fine river views on the way. Castelnau castle is eleventh-century, extended in the Hundred Years War, restored from 1896–1932. Once it had a garrison of 1,500 men and 100 horses. Its rent was then one egg a year, carried in pomp by four oxen to the Viscount of Turenne. It has super Aubusson and Beauvais tapestries (closed Tuesdays).

coloured tapestries, with a glass of white wine in your hand.

St-Céré is a perfect centre for touring the Dordogne, Lot and Quercy. They all meet here.

Food & Drink

Janine and the young Eric Bizat offer something for everybody. A judicious mixture of old re-gional Quercy dishes like carré de porc aux pruneaux (shoulder of pork with prunes) and not-too-extreme modern dishes like compôte de lapereau aux petits légumes (slowly stewed young rabbit with sli-vers of vegetables); four menus, all good value, a dish of the day announced ahead, specialities you must book ahead, speci-alities of the month, and season-al game specialities, including delicious pheasant with pears and a chartreuse de perdreau (braised partridge with bacon, sausage, cabbage and other veg-etables turned out of a mould).

On the cheapest menu, carré de porc is usually one of the main dish choices, with the dish of the day and stuffed tripe. The compôte de lapereau is a choice on the first course, so you can really have a Nouveau-Regional meal. But on the more expensive meals and the card are some of the great Quercy regional dishes, and I can recommend the way Eric prepares them. Salad of smoked goose in walnut oil, confit of duck and of goose, a sort of rich man's peasant dish of goose neck stuffed with foie gras, truffled omelette, cèpes omelette, salade aux cernaux (green unripe walnuts), and truffled goose and duck pâtés.

One lovely dish of which they are rightly proud is la tourtière de volaille aux ris de veau. A jointed chicken is rolled in flour and fried in goose fat. It is taken out, tomato, garlic and a glass of wine added to the juices and cooked. Back goes the chicken with the sweet-breads (ris de veau) chopped, herbs, and salsifis (long white root vegetable with a delicate flavour) blanched and chopped (if cèpes are in season, these are used instead). A cup of stock and oil is added and it is all cooked for ten minutes. Then flaky leaf pastry is put over the whole thing and it is put in a hot oven until the pastry is golden. It is very complicated – and absolutely delicious.

The very cheap red house wine here is called vin du Laboureur. The white is called Chez Nous. There is a superb list of Cahors reds – every year from 1975 to 1982 except 1977, with a choice of excellent Clos de Gamot and very good Château de Cayrou, both from Jean Jouffreau. There are half bottles of all but one wine, and a Cahors tasting seems in order if you are staying a few days.

If you do not fancy the strong, heavy Cahors, there is a fair list of Bordeaux and Beaujolais wines, as well as some good Burgundy. The choice of whites is rather limited but there are 1981 and 1979 Pouilly Fuissé at reasonable prices, so I would not look any further. Pouilly is one of those wines discovered by the Americans and can be overpriced. These are not.

La Pescalerie

La Pescalerie
Cabrerets, 46330 Lot (D662
then D41 E Cahors 34km).
Telephone: (65) 31.22.55.
Rooms F–G;
menus D (choice of two);
half-board G.
Closed 1 November to Palm
Sunday.
Visa, Amex, Diners.

French guides have called La Pescalerie 'Paradise on Earth' and 'God's House'. It is certainly one of the most alluring retreats from the noise, smells and harrying of town life I have found anywhere.

Two doctors gave up a clinic in Cahors to turn this remote eighteenth-century manor into a special haven. Hélène Combette runs the hotel and restaurant with calm and energy. Roger disappears each morning to his operating theatre in Cahors to mend the unlucky and the unwise, returns in the evening in time to fish in the little river Célé at the border of their land, take an apéritif with guests on the flowered terrace, and, still in his shirtsleeves and with jovial humour, serve food and wine in the dining room. It would be indelicate to ask if he also carved.

La Pescalerie is exquisitely furnished in antiques. The last bedroom I slept in had two 1½-size beds, a wardrobe big enough to take a royal flush of clothes, large chest, old desk, a table with four soft chairs, and there was still room to dance. On the beamed walls were original paintings, on the mantel a fine old clock stuck at half past twelve.

All bedrooms are different and all delightful. Those above have thick old beams meeting in an apex to hold up the roof. One I loved had a gallery up in its beams, and below two old curtained four-poster beds. The house has square towers, rows of dormer windows, a red roof and cream stone walls.

The grounds of La Pescalerie are also a joy. They run down from the terrace to the little river by way of colourful flower

beds, mature trees, lawns neatly cut but not shaved, dotted with daisies and a pillared rose walk leading to a statue of some forgotten beauty. Wisteria and roses climb the terrace wall and a spreading chestnut knocks on a bedroom window.

I feel here that I am a personal guest in a friend's country house. The French description 'la quietitude' is perfect.

Food & Drink

A real eighteenth-century kitchen is used for cooking at La Pescalerie. Dr Hélène used to do it all herself but now she has the help of René Sarre, who was taught by the great Michel Guérard. All the ingredients are fresh from the market except the vegetables, which are mostly grown in the garden.

The cooking has been described as *comme chez soi* – just like home – but I don't know many home cooks who could keep the natural flavour of ingredients like René Sarre does.

There is a 'suggestion' menu of five courses without a choice. Last time this was a salad from the garden with duck foie gras, a ragoût of artichokes and broad beans, guinea fowl sautéed with cabbage in tarragon, a superb local farm goat's cheese, and delicious apple tart. But I chose the dearer menu with some choice.

First course choices included a garden salad with cou d'oie farci – stuffed goose neck, a great old peasant dish of Dordogne-Quercy sliced like a sausage. An old local saying is: 'With the neck of a goose, bread and a bottle of wine, you can

*This is Quercy,
'Land of Prehistory',
where cavemen left behind
wall drawings and fossilized
footmarks. Just off D41 are the
Pech-Merle caves – vast
communicating caverns with
wall drawings of mammoths,
bison, deer, horses, human
hands and female bodies,
made 20,000 years ago,
stalagmite columns and bones
of cave-bears. They were
rediscovered in 1922 by two
schoolboys, though the vaults
had been used as a hideout in
the Revolution. (Open Palm
Sunday to 31 October.)*

*At Bouziès on D626 (5km)
high cliffs are riddled with
caves used by prehistoric
families. One, called Château
des Anglais, has a castellated
wall built by the English in the
Hundred Years War. Across
the Lot river at Bouziès on D40
is St-Cirq-La-Popie, village of
lovely old houses perched on
a rock, with superb views, a
fortified fifteenth-century
church and museum with
Ming period Chinese
treasures.*

*Near La Pescalerie a fountain
spouts from a rock wall – an
underground river surfacing.
Sauliac (6km) is a hamlet
clinging to a fearsome cliff
with openings to fortified
caves used for centuries as
war refuges. The fit climbed
ropes, the rest were hoisted in
baskets.*

*The route to Cahors (D41,
D662) gives fine views of the
river Lot. Cahors, in a
horseshoe bend of the Lot, has
many old buildings, including
a twelfth-century fortified*

*cathedral, and the fortified
medieval bridge, Valentré,
with three slim towers – one of
the world's most beautiful.*

*Have a look at the kitchen. It
is 18th century, beamed, with
old cookers still in use.*

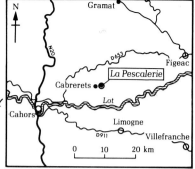

invite friends to a feast.' I ex-
perimented with vegetable
salad pied de veau (with cal-
ves' foot jelly) and found the
'pied' tasty but chewy.

Next course included a house
speciality – truite au bleu –
trout straight from the river
into boiling wine and vinegar
court-bouillon, turning it
slightly blue. But I had a gorg-
eously light puff confection
oozing Roquefort cheese. Then
I had a juicy cutlet of Causse
lamb

Among wickedly tempting
farm cheeses the Quercy Ca-
bécou of goat's milk won my
vote. The yellow Cantal with a
nutty flavour was splendid,
too.

It is difficult to resist the superb fruit tarts, but do try caramel ice with caramelized apples. It all sounds simple, but
you just have to taste it.

On the card, a chunk of foie
gras, goose or duck, is pricey,
as usual these days, and there
is a salad with delicious smoked fillets of goose. Otherwise
you gain little on the menus.

The breakfast croissant and
the jams are made by Hélène. A
big jug of coffee is placed over a
little heater to keep it hot.

The wine list is strong in good
Bordeaux wines but this is Cahors and the choice is excellent. A very drinkable AC is
fairly cheap, a superbly fruity,
smooth and full-flavoured Clos
de la Coutale is nearly three
times as much, and there are
plenty in between. Cahors is a
dark, strong wine with lots of
tannin which has suddenly become fashionable in Paris because it is one of the few wines
promoted to appellation contrôlée in recent years – 1971
(Gigondas is another). So its
price has shot up. A pity, because we were secret drinkers
of it for years. Long, long ago, it
was more popular with foreign
buyers in Bordeaux than the
local claret. It improves enormously with age – up to fifteen
years even. Other wines to look
for are Clos de Gamot, and
Château de Cayron. But ask Dr
Roger to advise you – he is an
expert.

LE VIEUX LOGIS

**Le Vieux Logis
Trémolat, Dordogne (post
24510 Ste Alvère), (34km
along the Dordogne river E of
Bergerac on D31).
Telephone (53) 22.80.06.
Rooms D–H;
menus B–E;
half-board F–H.
Closed January; restaurant
closed Tuesdays in winter.
Visa, Euro, Amex, Diners.**

Sheer delight! I have great admiration for the loving care, good taste and ideas of Mme Giraudel-Destord who has turned a rambling country logis into a charming and unusual hotel. And the young chef Didier Gélineau succeeds in reviving some of the great Périgourdine dishes with a light touch.

All rooms are furnished in fine antique pieces. The little salon by the foyer is comfortable, with an open fire for cooler days. The bar is cosy. The dining room is a joy – a fine old room with high-beamed ceiling and a beautiful balcony supported by old wooden pillars. The old garden of well-kept lawns, flowers and trees is a haven on a summer's day.

All the bedrooms are different, all furnished in old style. One I coveted in the main house had lovely old beams, an open fire, and a bed in an alcove with curtains to pull across. Mine was in the converted stables. The room was very pleasant with old furniture, wallpaper of rustic eighteenth-century scenes, a modern bath-room and separate loo, which I like. The bed was very wide and deep and was covered with a huge eiderdown so thick I could have drowned in it. Alas, other guests passed my ground floor window, so I had to pull the curtains. I hate that, but I could hardly inflict my podgy body on the public.

The service was willing and good, especially that of the young people in the dining room, who spoke English.

Trémolat village is so French that Claude Chabrol chose it as the setting for his film Le Boucher. It has a strange decaying fortified church. This is not the most attractive part of the Dordogne, except for Cingle de Trémolat (loop) near the village. You see this best from Belvedere Rocamadou, 3km past the village. The river swings through a semi-circle of high bare white cliffs, joined by bridges of golden stone. Rowing and canoeing regattas are held here, and a water-sports centre is nearby.

LOCAL DRIVES

Cross the Dordogne at Trémolat and follow D28, D29, D37 along the river towards Bergerac to Lanquais Castle, 15km (open 1 April to 31 October; closed Tuesdays). Tower remains from medieval castle destroyed by the English in the Hundred Years War. The rest was built over centuries in different styles. Nice Louis XIII (early seventeenth-century) furniture and French ceilings.

Take D51 east of Limeuil (meeting the Vézère and Dordogne rivers), cross the Dordogne at Le Buisson on to D25, then back again at Siorac on to D703 to Beynac – attractive riverside village with restaurants (try Hôtel Bonnet) and good fishing and river views. On a rock above is an historic castle. It was the French frontline in the Hundred Years War (1337–1453), deadly enemy of Castelnaud across the river held by the English. Raiding parties met and fought often. (Open 1 March to 5 November). Interesting , superb panorama from the watch walk, but little furniture in it.

I am frequently given rooms in converted stables, and I do eat like a horse. But where will the horses sleep when the oil runs out.?

Food & Drink

Chef Didier Gélineau believes that everything possible should be fresh, including the bread which he bakes himself, from the rolls to the walnut bread and raisin bread served with cheese.

He also believes in traditional Périgordian cooking with a light modern touch, and his card contains some delicious local dishes. They include tourain (often called tourin), which is onion, tomato and

milk soup, thickened with egg yolk, poured over bread and sprinkled with cheese; a delicious duck liver terrine; pommes Sarladaises – a luxury potato dish of baked sliced potatoes with truffles; superb cèpes, the delicate mushrooms, cooked slowly in oil, served with parsley, garlic and shallots (à la persillade); veal fillet cooked in garlic; oeufs brouillés aux truffes – scrambled egg speckled with truffle pieces; and truffes en feuilleté – whole truffles in puff pastry. Alas, truffles are dearer than ever now.

I tried a classic of Périgueux – cuisse de canard confit à l'ancienne (drumstick of duck preserved in duckfat in a pot) and it was truly done in the 'ancient' traditional way and served with delicious fresh vegetables. This dish was on the second cheapest menu, the alternative being veal in garlic. Didier offers four menus, from a pleasant four-course menu with no choice to a Menu Dégustation for two people. You must add fifteen per cent service to all prices – it is *non compris*.

Before my confit, I chose truite de mer (salmon trout, which is like a more delicate salmon), deliciously cooked in a court bouillon and served in a wine and slightly-creamed sauce, almost certainly made with the court-bouillon stock and with just enough lemon juice to bring out the fish's flavour. Many chefs, even very good ones, use too much lemon in fish sauces.

Despite a tempting cheeseboard, with good Quercy and Auvergne cheeses, I picked fromage de chèvre chaud (grilled goat cheese) served with a nut-oil salad with pieces of chopped walnut. I love it.

Didier's desserts are imaginative and light. He uses the traditional local drink, old prune brandy, effectively, including in a punch glacé, a frothy water ice of wine and egg whites to which rum is usually added. There is also an airy hot pastry with cream of ginger and caramelized pear.

All this is served in a charming dining room with high arched and beamed ceiling and balustraded wooden balcony supported by wooden posts. Very much like a medieval hall.

The wine list is sensibly chosen, not too long but ranging from a very-drinkable Bergerac La Borderie blanc de blancs to Lafite and Mouton Rothschild and a superb Cheval Blanc, king of St Emilion.

Bergerac wines suffer by comparison with their Bordeaux neighbours and in my view are under-estimated. Several AC (appellation contrôlée) wines are produced round Bergerac and they are good value. It is the reds which are most underestimated, and Vieux Logis has two of the best on its list – Domaine du Haut Pécharmant and Château Les Pradets. They are rather similar to an ordinary AC St Emilion – the nearest Bordeaux area.

Monbazillac, the sweet Dordogne wine once considered a rival to Sauternes, has improved again and, like Sauternes, makes a splendid first drink around 11.30a.m., or goes well with strong cheese. Château Treuil de Nailhac, on this list, is one of the very best.

PARIS–
LYON
INCLUDING
BURGUNDY

Auberge de la Scierie
La Vove, Aix-en-Othe, 10160
Aube (4km S of N60 Sens-
Troyes road, 39km past Sens).
Telephone: (25) 46.71.26.
Rooms D;
menus B, D;
half-board D.
Closed December, January,
part February; restaurant
closed Monday evenings and
Tuesdays in winter except for
people staying.
Visa, Amex, Diners.

Imagine a West Country inn with dormer windows and porches, creeper clad, in an enchanting garden with a trout river running through; add a swimming pool, French ambience and French cooking and you have a hotel which rates, for us, far above its two stars.

It is one of the most enchanting little hotels we know in France. Pathways through the grounds take you to little bridges over the river, stone seats, and a pair of resident swans. Eating or drinking in the garden is a delight in the right weather.

Inside are open fires for chilly days, comfortable furniture, and patterned Laura Ashley style wallpapers, except in the dining room, where old tools of country trades and pictures of old country scenes decorate the walls, and huge bellows decorate the ceiling.

The bedrooms in two long pavilions in the garden are very pretty. They are all on the ground floor. Ours had French windows to the swimming pool and windows overlooking the river. It has a separate entrance hall, separate wc and shower, green carpet, pretty pink velvet armchair and pink and green flowers on the frilly bedlinen, delightful etchings and watercolours on the wall and a copper etching of a sixteenth-century vendage.

The hotel was once a sawmill, and an old steam saw still stands in the banqueting room, with an old cider press. Alas, the patron M. Duguet does not make his own cider. He serves it in the dining room, though. This area, Othe, is cider country and there has been a great rebirth of cider-making recently, with apple trees replacing vines. In 1919 they made ten million bottles.

To regulars from the local area the Scierie is called 'La Joyeuse' and it is certainly a happy, captivating place to eat and stay.

You can learn how to rear goats and make goats cheese on a short activity holiday. Others include wood-carving and horse riding.

There are horses to ride. The river Nosle is pretty and there are walks alongside it and in the woods around Aix-en-Othe. The market in Aix is on Wednesday and Saturday mornings.

Food & Drink

There are salmon and trout in the waters round here, and both appear on the hotel's card. In season, salmon dishes are the house speciality and, if it is on the card or the menus, I would order it. It is served either 'feuilleté' (in flaky pastry) or 'en papillotte' (baked in aluminium foil). Either way, it is stuffed with cooked sorrel and served with a superb cream of asparagus sauce in season, or a delicious sauce made of shallot cooked in white wine, vermouth and fish stock, reduced to a syrup, then thickened further with fresh cream and cooked sorrel. The foil in which the salmon is served is shaped like a swan.

On the dearer menu, salmon is a second course choice and so is trout in hazelnuts, so it is a little difficult to know which to choose. The first course usually includes another house speciality, home-made rabbit (lapereau) terrine covered in hazelnuts.

After the fish course they serve a trou ('a hole') of apple sorbet in Calvados. It is remarkable how this does settle my digestion and make me ready to face a main course, even if I have been tasting too many good restaurant meals lately.

On the main course I like veal kidneys braised in Cham-

pagne. Barbara recommends filet au parfum de morilles – beautiful fillet steak cooked with diced morilles, those delicate fungi which bring out the flavour of a dish more subtly than mushrooms, served with tiny portions of four vegetables.

You can then have a strong local goat's milk cheese (Crottin d'Othe) grilled, which I love, or a choice of fifteen cheeses, including Troyes (sometimes called Barbery), a soft cheese rather like Camembert, Chaource, creamier and richer, Autun, a cow's milk cheese from just over the Burgundy border, Maroilles, a sharper version of Carré de l'Est of Champagne.

Pâtisseries are above average, but I go for another sorbet, called Colonel. You have a lemon sorbet and a bottle of vodka to pour what you will over it. Barbara liked vacherin glacé au coulis de fraises – a meringue ring filled with ice-cream, whipped cream and strawberries with a strawberry sauce.

A choice in the cheap menu is a home-made boudin or a sir-

loin steak in a sauce of Auvergne blue cheese. The duck foie gras on the card is home-made.

The wine list shows bottle labels and prices. The house red is a Côtes du Rhône, and there is a fairly good choice of reds, including a low price Grande Versanne Bordeaux and a nice 1982 Gigondas. I did expect a better choice of Burgundy and of white. The Chablis and Sancerre are good, and appropriately pricey, and the Alsace Riesling over-priced. The temptation is to pay up and buy yourself a Champagne Nature Chardonnay, a still Champagne officially called Coteaux Champenois these days. The amount made is strictly controlled, you don't find it far away from the Champagne, and this might be a chance to try it. I prefer a really good Chablis, but that is a matter of taste. In fact, we settled for a worthy, if rather dull, Alexis Lichine Graves at a reasonable price and that did not spoil our enjoyment of good food, nice atmosphere and friendly service.

 LOCAL DRIVES Sens (39km) and
Château Fleurigny
(N60 to Villeneuve
l'Archevêque then D28, D25 –
37km) – see Hostellerie du
Moulin, Flagy, page 103.

Troyes (31km) – on the Seine,
once capital of the
Champagne and a centre of
art, it is now much
industrialized, but still retains
its old streets, churches and
gabled houses. Here, in 1420,
Isabeau, wife of the mad
Charles VI, left Paris, made
Troyes her capital, and signed
a treaty with England's Henry
V. She disinherited the
Dauphin; Henry married her
daughter Catherine, and
became Regent, then King of
France as well as England. He
was married in the cathedral
of St Peter and St Paul, which
was started in 1208, took four
centuries to build, and still
lacks one tower. It is a
beautiful Gothic building,
ornately sculptured, with
thirteenth- and sixteenth-
century windows of intense
colours showing bible scenes
and popes. The window
showing Christ and a wine
press is most macabre.

Lac et Forêt d'Orient (21km E
of Troyes on N19) is a huge
lake which was man-made in
1965 to regulate the flow of the
Seine. It lies in a pleasant
forest. There's sailing at
Mesnil St Pierre; and an
animal reserve in the forest
with wild boar and deer.

Tonnerre (59km) and
Renaissance châteaux of
Tanlay and Ancy-le-Franc –
see Moulin de Pommerats,
Venizy, St Florentin, page 113.

Chez Camille

Chez Camille
1, place Edouard-Herriot,
Arnay-le-Duc, 21230 Côte
d'Or (on N6, 10 mins from A6
motorway at Pouilly-en-
Auxois).
Telephone: (80) 90.01.38.
Rooms E;
menus A, B.
Closed 15 to 25 January;
restaurant closed Sunday
evenings.
Visa, Euro, Amex, Diners.

An endearing little hotel with genuinely warm welcome and outstanding cuisine. Armand and Monique Poinsot have entirely renovated a sixteenth-century house with flair and thought. It is comfortable, pleasant and quiet, despite being on the N6 road. Little to criticize except that the pretty lounge with a big fireplace and wicker furniture is small, so are some bedrooms.

They are reached by an original sixteenth-century staircase of oak and red tiles. Ours had a sloping roof with beam, charming blue and grey décor, and huge Louis XV wardrobe. There was a glass jar of sweets awaiting us. Such temptations are hardly fair. The bathroom was pleasant, with tiled floor and floral tiled walls, and the WC separate.

The restaurant is captivating. Made by putting a glass roof over the courtyard, it has stone walls and floors, warm wood beams, comfortable wicker armchairs, flowers and trellis-work. By day you see the blue sky, by night you dine by the light of street lanterns and candles. They even put up umbrellas when the sun shines. The kitchen is behind the glass in the corner of the dining room.

There is a sauna for guests and also a UVA solarium which costs 100F an hour to use.

Arnay-le-Duc is a little old town of pointed towers and turrets like the backcloth for a fairy story. Tour de la Motte-Forte is the remains of a fifteenth-century château, owned by the Princes of Condé.

Food & Drink

Both menus here are good value, especially in view of Armand Poinsot's outstanding cooking. He offers a choice of richer Burgundian dishes and lighter dishes such as a fresh salmon tartare on the card, which is not dear.

Both menus include a large carafe of red wine and coffee. On the cheaper menu, I had scrambled eggs with truffles in preference to the soup, followed by the 'dish of the market', which was magret of duck (not too underdone), served

Beaune (35km) and Burgundy wine road – see entry under Moulin d'Hauterive, page 109.

Châteauneuf – take N81 NE towards Pouilly-en-Auxois for 11km, right on D994 through Rouvre, under the motorway, to Iles Bordes, then a small road right to a château. Built in the twelfth century, it stayed in the Châteauneuf family until 1456 when Catherine de Châteauneuf killed her husband with poisoned cakes. A kitchen maid stole one and died, too, so Catherine's crime was discovered. She was drawn on a hurdle through the streets of Paris and burned at the stake. The Château is closed on Tuesdays. It stands in a photogenic fortified village.

Château de Sully is easily missed; take D36 S from Arnay to Epinac, then turn right on little roads D24F, D26 – 24km. Not to be confused with

Château de Sully on the Loire, nor has it any connection with Henry IV's minister, Sully. It is magnificent. A Renaissance building, it has had several additions. You can visit only the outside and the vast park, from the Saturday before Palm Sunday until 30 September.

Autun (28km S) was one of Europe's most important cities in Roman days. Now a quiet spot, visited mostly for its great twelfth-century cathedral, containing many treasures, including the strange but beautiful sculptural ensembles by Gilbert (Gislebertus) in the twelfth-century.

La Rochepot (just off N6, 24km SE) is a pretty village with hilltop medieval castle (open daily except Tuesdays from Palm Sunday to 1 November).

Morvan Regional Park (NW) is very lovely; see entry under Moulin des Ruats, Avallon, page 106.

with bilberries, apple slices, mushrooms, potato slices and piped purée of chestnut round the edge of the plate. Then came cream cheese with fines herbes or sugar or a choice of desserts.

The card has some delightful and unusual dishes. Despite such temptations as halibut soup, Burgundy snails, and a splendid hot oyster dish, my choice is the shoulder of wild boar in wine jelly – Burgundy wine, of course.

The main dishes include raw Charolais steak tartare cut in thin slices, an interesting civet of eels (lamproie) sliced, cooked in red wine with leeks and garlic, and the blood used to thicken the sauce – an old Bordelaise recipe; and an expensive but excellent 'fish tasting' (dégustation de poissons) in four courses, called la belle marée. My choice is typical of Burgundy but less enterprising – fillet of beef in truffle juice en croûte (in pastry).

The cheeseboard has a wide choice of the fine Burgundy cheeses. The desserts are inventive, some rich and some pleasingly alcoholic. An unusual mixture was a mousse of chocolate and griottes, which are rather sharp red cherries.

Armand is a true wine lover, has big cellars and will willingly let you see them. His wine list is mouthwatering but rather heavily loaded towards dearer finer wines. Great Burgundies are outrageously expensive. So he has picked some of the best 'good' wines.

There is a splendid choice of Côtes-de-Beaune and Côtes-de-Nuits reds, plus seventeen different Burgundy whites,

rising to a very pricey 1957 Mercurey La Mission. Only a drop of white Mercurey is made; it is like a cross between Montrachet and Mersault. Further, there is a long list of older, finer, pricier Bordelais.

For tighter budgets, there is a well-chosen list of Beaujolais. I can recommend his Lacoque Morgon 1980, just old enough to show its strength and individuality. The unmistakable smell of a good Morgon has created a word in France — morgonner. This wine goes very well with that Charolais steak tartare, or my filet en croûte. In fact I paid double for a Beaune. I picked one which I had never tried, a 1979 Domaine des Pierres Blanches. It was a bit young, perhaps, but already surprisingly full-bodied and satisfying.

The 1979 Montagny Bertrand white wine was a full, heavy wine, fairly priced. But if you fancy a good Burgundy white at a not-outrageous price, try the Chassagne Montrachet from Marcel Picard Château de la Maltroye 1979. That is a good age for a Chassagne, which can be drunk even younger. This full, smooth wine will suit most palates.

If you like a really smooth dry white, with a most pleasant flowery after-taste, there is a delicious Mersault here from Les Charmes. It would convert a non-wine drinker to dry white wine. Experts call it 'feminine', but a lot of girls I know are a lot harder and sharper than Les Charmes. I must not say less charming.

A haven for wine lovers — only 35 km from Beaune.

Hostellerie du Château de Bellecroix

Hostellerie du Château de Bellecroix
71150 Chagny, Saône-et-Loire (on N6, 2km S of Chagny on way to Châlon-sur-Saône; 15km from Beaune on N14; 15km from A6 motorway sortie Beaune or Châlon Nord).
Telephone: (85) 87.13.86.
Rooms C–G;
menus A, B.
Closed Wednesday and 20 December to 1 February.
Visa, Amex, Diners.

A fairy-tale château, creeper-clad, with two pointed round towers, set back in a five-acre park away from traffic of N6. A peaceful, comfortable and reasonably-priced base for Beaune, Châlon and the wine roads of Burgundy. The excellent cooking is a bonus.

An old Commanderie of the Knights of St John from 1199, it combines beautifully twelfth- and eighteenth-century architecture. In the park is a fifteenth-century cross. One side shows Christ with a cross of Malta in his halo, the other shows the Virgin. The building has survived intact, partly because some of its walls are seven feet (two metres) thick.

Mme Gauthier bought the castle only six years ago and with the help of her husband, has certainly made it into an elegant and endearing hotel. There is a lovely spiral staircase and four of the fifteen bedrooms are round rooms in the towers. They are prettily furnished. The dining room is huge, panelled in carved wood, with a huge stone fireplace.

Food & Drink

One famous French gastronomic magazine described young Armand Lollini's gratin de saumon au fenouil as 'worthy of a sonnet'. A little lyrical, but Armand can certainly cook and is on his way up in the world of French cuisine. Cleverly, he uses all the cunning decorative effects and colour in dishes of Nouvelle Cuisine, but if you look closely at his repertoire it is mostly straightforward, old-style French cooking – and none the worse for that.

He does not have a long card, but offers 'proposals' based on the market each day. When we were there these included a splendid gratin of queues de langoustines – scampi tails in a cream sauce, browned under the grill, and served here with fèves – broad beans. One reason why broad beans are so much nicer in France is that they often skin them as well as podding them. It makes them sweeter.

Barbara had the cheap menu, which was a bargain. No choice, however. She started with a salad with chicken livers and croûtons, then had a very tasty chicken with baby vegetables, a good choice of Burgundy cheeses and, as dessert, four different sorbets – lemon, peach, blackcurrant and strawberry, with two sauces and sliced kiwi fruit.

In the dearer, but not very dear, menu I was offered a rather odd dish of poached egg in curry and boiled egg, or an excellent terrine of white chicken meat persillé – in a parsley jelly.

The main course was that gratin of salmon with fennel which deserves a sonnet or jambonnette de canard à la graine de moutarde, a sort of duck 'sausage' in a sauce of grain mustard. Then cheese and a small choice of desserts of which I thought the assortment of sorbets the nicest. But then I do not like chocolate gâteau, and that is the speciality.

Armand Lollini is only thirty-three, which is young for a chef. He is slightly under the shadow of the great three-star *Michelin* restaurant in a fine old Bourguignone house in Chagny, Lameloise, where the only menu dégustation costs more than twice the Bellecroix's dearest menu, and the card a lot more still. But Armand is a graduate of a great school – Strasbourg hotel school – he has enormous talent, and if he would concentrate a little more on the great regional dishes of Strasbourg and Burgundy, he would be one of the best.

The wine list has to be nearly all Burgundy and it is a very tempting list; nothing too exotic, although I would not com-

LOCAL DRIVES Chagny itself is a quiet little industrial town and centre of gastronomy. A Fair of table wines is held in mid-August. Here starts the Côte d'Or wine area. The N74 road to Beaune and Dijon, with side roads, reads like a great wine list. It starts with Montrachet, then Meursault, and so on through Beaune (see entry under Moulin d'Hauterive, St-Gervais-en-Vallière, page 109), Nuits St Georges, Vougeot, Chambolle, Gevrey-Chambertin to Dijon itself.

I love Dijon. Known now for its restaurants and mustard, it was the capital of the Dukes of Burgundy who, in the fifteenth-century, ruled as much land as the Kings of France and were as powerful. The centre of the city is place de la Libération, formerly place Royale, designed in the seventeenth century by Mansart, who designed Versailles. The Ducal Palace is suitably imposing and sumptuous and contains a splendid Museum de Beaux Arts. Dijon has a superb Foire Gastronomique (Gastronomic Fair) in the first two weeks of November. I have fine memories and loss of memories of it. A sensible arrangement is that you buy a little mallet (now plastic). If you see someone you fancy, you tap them on the head with it. They can walk away, which is the end of the affair, tap you back, which means that you have a chance, or grab your mallet, which means that you are in. When I was young I started on a tour of the streets, wine tasting and mallet-tapping, after dinner and found myself having breakfast, sitting on the edge of a fountain which was filled with red wine, with a girl whom I did not remember ever having seen before but who seemed to know me very well. It was a good breakfast – sausage from a stall opposite and free wine.

South from Chagny is another wine area – Côte Chalonnaise – which is worth exploring, too. Take N481 south. Wine villages are on the side roads. Here are: Rully, home of sparkling Burgundy and also some good still white; Mercurey, where you should wander the vineyard lanes; Givry, an historic little town with some fine buildings. Henry IV's mistress, Gabrielle d'Estrées, after staying at a nearby château, introduced Henry to Givry wine and he became so addicted that he kept it on his dining table and exempted it from duty. The duty soon had to be put back because almost every wine in Paris was suddenly marked 'Givry'. The Côte Chalonnaise finishes with Buxy and Montagny, but drive on – you are in Mâcon and then Beaujolais.

plain at all if someone treated me to the Louis Trapet 1978 Chambertin. Not Gevrey-Chambertin, but the veritable Chambertin itself, and Trapet makes a near-perfect wine. Remember what Hilaire Belloc said about confessing his sins to St Peter: 'I am sorry, St Peter. I cannot remember the name of the village in France, I cannot remember the name of the girl, nor even what we had for dinner. But, my God, the wine was Chambertin!'

There are some beautiful white wines on the list – Montrachets, Mersaults from leading producers. But if you want something different and somewhat cheaper try the Mercurey Château de Chamirey 1981. Little white Mercurey is made. I find it rather akin to Montrachet – smooth and firm – but Barbara does not like it. She likes the much cheaper Rully non-sparkler from the best producer, Delorme. There is a 1982 on this list.

The red Burgundy list runs from a simple Passetoutgrain (a blend of Gamay and Pinot Noir grapes) to the Chambertin and a Château Pommard. Among the cheaper wines is an 1982 red Mercurey. A lot of Frenchmen love this wine but although I like its iron and its body, I find it rough and earthy. So here is your chance to see if Henry IV was right about Givry. There is a good one – 1981 Cellier aux Moines from Delorme. It is lighter than Mercurey; it is delicate, very fruity and has a flowery smell. I like it very much. Henry IV was right. It would make a very royal daily plonk.

A wine-bibber's paradise – on two Burgundy wine roads, only 15 km from Beaune.

Hostellerie du Moulin

**Hostellerie du Moulin
Flagy, near Montereau-faut-
Yonne; post 77156 Thoury
Ferottes, Seine-et-Marne.
Telephone: (6) 096.67.89.
Rooms single B to C; double D
to F breakfast included.
menus A, B (choice of two)
Closed 9–21 September, 20–24
December, Sunday evenings,
Mondays.**

Take someone you love – or aspire to love. A superb rustic hideaway with atmosphere and charm.

I turned right on to the D120 from the fussy, rattly N6 from Fontainebleau to Sens (still marked N5 on my map), through the village of Noisy where nothing moved, and was through the village of Flagy without seeing even a hotel sign. Returning, I stopped by the bridge over the river Orvanne. In a stone lavatoire below two women were washing clothes. Further down, the water ran under an old building. The mill – Hostellerie du Moulin. Outside were lawns to the river under willows. Inside, a bar in simple village style, a charming dimly lit beamed lounge surrounding mill wheels and pulleys, and a light dining room looking out to lawns, with huge log fire for winter. You can eat under the willows in summer

Up steep stairs were ten bedrooms with beams, some with stone walls, old country furniture and last-century prints – all different, in good simple

taste and with good modern bathrooms. My massive bed was comfortable – and lonely! Doors shivered and floorboards creaked eerily, befitting a thirteenth-century mill which was still grinding corn until 1950. There is nothing chi-chi about the conversion to a hotel.

Claude Scheidecker, his wife and staff run it efficiently but with real consideration and friendliness. Refugees from industrial Montereau across the N6 escape here for dinner, Sunday lunch, or in small groups for 'business' meals. When they have gone, all is quiet except for the creak of old wood and trickle of the gently running river.

Do walk round Flagy. It's a true old farming village, with footbridges over the river to front doors and a main square with a dignified *mairie* fit for 1914 call-up proclamations, a church, two old-style village shops, one selling bread, wine and vegetables, the other selling everything, and a corner bar-café where men sit around playing cards or dominoes and put their drinks on the slate.

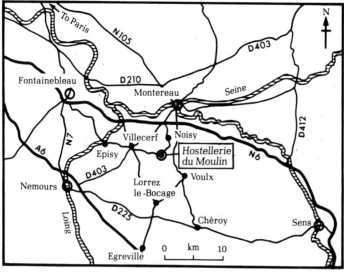

French throne. It was agreed that for all time France and England were to have the same King. Somewhere later the crown slipped.

For Château Fleurigny, take N6 towards Sens and turn left on D25. On banks of the Oreuse river, surrounded by water, it is a grand but severe Renaissance house between fourteenth-century towers, with grey walls plunging into the moat. The inside courtyard is charming, with first floor arcaded galleries and the beautiful chapel has works by Jean Cousin, Renaissance painter on wood and glass whose work on perspective influenced many great painters.

In Sens, in Burgundy, the old town's ramparts have become boulevards and walks. The cathedral of St Etienne, started 1140, was the first great Gothic cathedral of France and its master mason William of Sens went to Canterbury to rebuild the chancel. The medieval stained glass is splendid. One twelfth-century window shows the murder at Canterbury of Thomas à Becket, once in exile nearby. There are priceless vestments, goblets and tapestries in the cathedral treasury.

![LOCAL DRIVES]

Paris 85km. Château de Fontainebleau (23km) – historically the most interesting of Royal châteaux, altered or partly rebuilt by nearly all French monarchs and by Napoleon, who loved it and abdicated there in 1814. Follow the forest road N837 (lovely walks) to Milly-la-Forêt, charming little town with market halls of oak and restored twelfth-century chapel with decoration by the writer, poet and artist Jean Cocteau, buried there in 1963.

Montereau (10km across N6) is industrial but historically important. The Seine and Yonne meet here. Nearby, Ile de France meets the Champagne and Burgundy. In 1419, on the bridge over the Yonne, Jean the Fearless, Duke of Burgundy, met the Armagnac supporters of the French Dauphin to form an alliance against the English under Henry V, hero of Agincourt. The Armagnacs treacherously assassinated Jean on the bridge, Henry joined with Burgundy, married the King of France's daughter, and became Regent of France and heir to the

Delightful water mill far from any busy road.

Royal love-nest! still fit for a King.

Food & Drink

Regis Durand, chef of the Moulin, flirts with Nouvelle Cuisine but is not married to it! For instance, Nouvelle's compulsory magret de canard (nearly raw duck's breast) is on the card but in a sauce of blackcurrant berries, not raspberry vinegar. The menus are good value and you might well find the dishes I mention on them.

Last time I tried praires à l'Anis – clams out of the shell grilled with aniseed (probably pastis). Pleasant, but a little gritty. I prefer the house speciality – coquilles St Jacques au Noilly (scallops in vermouth sauce) served on a bed of spinach.

Fillet of beef with a blue cheese sauce (bleu de Causses) served with pâtes fraîches (pasta) is delightful, but do try first the fricassée de rognons et ris de veau – veal kidneys and sweetbreads deliciously cooked in cider and chervil; soft, delicate and very tasty.

The cheeseboard has six different Bries – local Montereau (sharp), Mulen (sweeter, stronger smelling), Coulomniers (enriched with cream), Fougères, Grotte-paille, and the great Meaux fermier, called the true King of Cheeses by Talleyrand. Taste them all. Poems have been written to Brie for centuries in France.

The chef's special dessert is caramelized pear, but the Moulin is also known for delicious pâtisserie and I have had a lovely light pear tart.

The wine list is well chosen. The house white, a palatable Sauvignon of Loir-et-Cher, is remarkably good value. With kidneys, I had a very pleasant red Graves, but with the kidneys, the fillet and certainly the Brie, the house carafe red would go nicely. I tried a quarter carafe with the Brie. It is a Beaujolais Village. Much as I love really good and great wines, I am not going to pass up value like the house white and red here in a Château Hôtel Indépendant. Mind you, if with someone you are aspiring to love, the Gevrey-Chambertin might be worth it.

The food is good and good value.

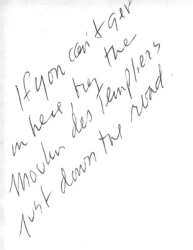

If you can't get in here try the Moulin des Templiers just down the road.

Hostellerie du Moulin des Ruats
Vallée du Cousin, 89200
Avallon, Yonne (5km SW of
Avallon by D427; Avallon is
on N6, 8km to motorway A6).
Telephone: (86) 34.07.14.
Rooms B–D;
menu C;
card C, D.
Closed 25 October to 4 March;
Monday, Tuesday lunch.
Visa, Euro, Amex, Diners.

Take a lover who also loves fishing!

A ravishing old flour mill with flower-decked balconies hidden in a secretive steep lush green valley, alongside the little river Cousin. In summer you can eat on the river bank in the shade of trees and within casting distance of the trout.

A more modern building attached to provide a delightful dining room and extra bedrooms is creeper clad and decorated and furnished within as if it is part of the mill. It remains unabashed by illustrious neighbours – the two-star *Michelin* Poste in Avallon described by *Gault Millau* as 'a paradise of French gastronomy and hotellerie' and L'Espérance down the road to Vézelay, another restored mill with three *Michelin* stars, 4 toques and 19 out of 20 from *Gault Millau*.

Des Ruats may not quite match them for cuisine or smooth super-service but it is quieter, cheaper, prettier, more relaxed, in more beautiful surroundings and appeals not only to us but to locals from Avallon who tend to fill the dining room. So book ahead. It has had a good reputation since long before the last war. The present happy owner, Yves Luciani, was maître d'hôtel for twenty-five years until he took over in 1982. He and his wife, Geneviève, will give you a charming welcome.

The beamed and wood-panelled dining room overlooking the river has old farmhouse furniture. There is a lounge and bar in the old mill. So was our bedroom, which had flowery wallpaper, rustic furniture, lot of lights, a nice pink bathroom and a small balcony.

A hotel of simple, comfortable charm, for a quiet rest or for an overnight stop away from the motorway.

Food & Drink

There are trout fishermen along the banks and on the little bridges of the river Cousin, and it is not surprising that trout tops the main course on the only menu – La truite au bleu 'Major Thompson'. Now, the good Major is a French fictional Englishman, with bowler hat, striped pants, rolled umbrella

This is the Morvan which deserves to be better known. A land of green hills, quiet valleys, trout rivers and lakes with the A6 motorway through the middle, taking the heavy traffic. A land to wander almost aimlessly, stopping where you will and not worrying about time. The Moulin is a fine base.

Avallon, built on a spur of rock, has ramparts, a twelfth-century church and superb views from its park. It is the northern gateway to Morvan Regional Park. But for drama Avallon pales beside Vézelay, 13km W. You see its hilltop towers from Fontette on the road from Avallon, sometimes appearing to float in a sea of cloud covering the valley. As you reach the town, you park and walk up the steep main street between jostling houses to the main square and the basilica of Sainte Madeleine. To me, this view is disappointing after the vision of beauty from afar. Despite the towers, it has a flat look, and some restored sculptures look like imitations. The inside is glorious. Architects go into raptures about its harmony, the devout say that it fills them with spiritual joy. I love the figures on the capitals telling stories from the Bible, and of lust, greed, despair, and of the Devil himself. Some are quite funny – deliberately, I am sure. Behind the basilica is a terrace with a wide view of Morvan. From here, in 1146, St Bernard preached and persuaded Louis VII and his followers, gathered on the slopes below, into going on the disastrous Second Crusade, and here, in 1190, Richard Lionheart of England and Louis Auguste of France, arch enemies, met to set off together on the Third Crusade. Restoring this church was the first major restoration job of Villet-le-Duc. Happily he had not yet developed his bad habit of adding extra spires and other items, as in Périgueux and other places. Wander any of the roads southwards or NE from Avallon up to the Château at Montbard and you will find one little treasure after another.

and army moustache. I assume that the trout is called after him because it is true blue.

Barbara chose the menu and thought the trout good. First she had a very good fish mousse with three sauces, all spiced. She chose fromage blanc à la crème in preference to a board covered in all those lovely Burgundy cheeses, and raspberries in preference to the house crêpe or soufflé. It seemed to me that she was having a nasty attack of slimming.

A French guide has called this menu too dear, and I agree that most hotels like this would offer both fish and meat on such a menu. But the card prices are average for this type of hotel, with some dishes cheaper.

I was delighted to find on the card a space headed 'Aujourd-'hui, le Chef propose:' And after a surfeit of chefs proposing I had duck breasts in raspberry vinegar or ris de veau (sweetbreads), it was a joy to have this chef of Le Moulin offering me coq au vin Bourguignon – a genuine old-fashioned chicken cooked in red Burgundy wine and served with a choice of fresh vegetables. It was like finding a genuine, beautifully cooked steak and kidney pie after living off delicate cocktail

snacks. Furthermore, among the dishes were that lightly-smoked sweet Morvan ham, served raw, the trout from the river on the fish course, and a gorgeous strong Vézelay goat's cheese. And if the chef does not happen to be proposing coq au vin, there is always fillet steak or grilled rib. For this is the original Charolais cattle country.

Moulin des Ruats may not be for gourmets, but it is splendid for gourmands.

It comes as a bit of a shock when you look on a wine list for a Vin de la Région and find it is something like a Blanc de Blancs Champagne, as happened to me on the Epernay road. In this case it is Chablis, which is just north of here (choice of one premier cru, Fourchaume, and three grand cru, Valmur, Les Blanchots and Vaudésir). The regional red and rosé are less ambitious but there's a very quaffable Bourgogne appellation contrôlée from Épineuil. These and the red Coulanges also on the list are some of the best Yonne AC wines.

The list of Burgundy wines, white and red, is splendid, and once again it depends on personal taste and price as to which you choose. One which is little known outside Burgundy is Monthélie, rather like

a Volnay but it matures quicker. A tip about Beaune – Bouchard Père et Fils put some of their very best wines into a premier cru blend called Beaune du Château. It is excellent, good value and top of the Burgundy red wine list.

The best Beaune white wine is offered – Corton–Charlemagne, also from Bouchard. It has a superb Chardonnay smell, slightly nutty, lots of flavour and strength.

A nice touch – the good list of Champagne is headed Vins de Joie. Champagne certainly brings joy to me.

Moulin d'Hauterive
St Gervais-en-Vallière, postal
address – 71350 Verdun-sur-
le-Doubs, Saône-et-Loire (in
hamlet of Chaublanc, 3km NE
of St Gervais, 15km from
Beaune and A6 motorway
Beaune exit).
Telephone: (85) 91.55.56.
Rooms E;
apartments G;
menus A (tourist), D
(gastronomic);
half-board E.
Closed December, January;
Sunday evenings, Mondays
out of season.
Visa, Euro, Amex, Diners.

The only sound you will hear at night in this magnificently-furnished old oil mill is of the little river Dheune tumbling over a weir – then only if you have a room overlooking the river where it washes the hotel's walls. It is in open country, among fields, yet only 15km from beautiful but bustling Beaune, and the wine road of Burgundy which reads like a glorious wine list. The mill was built in the twelfth century, largely reconstructed in the seventeenth and sympathetically converted into a hotel, keeping its original solid elegance with high windows and dormers in the roof. The green creeper climbing its cream stone walls turns vivid red in autumn.

It has eight acres of garden and park, with fishing, tennis court, horses to ride and a sauna for recovering from such exertions.

The whole hotel is beautifully furnished in antique style with refined taste. Every room has exposed beams and even the top rooms with sloping ceilings have space. Everything is done to give an effect of warmth and light. Our room had one wall painted white, another covered with a striped carpet. We had a huge arm-chair, TV and minibar. The warm carpeted bathroom had mauve bath, basin, bidet and wc. One bedroom has a lovely low four-poster with striped awnings.

The comfortable main lounge has a big open fire, and so has the attractive dining room, cosy despite old stone walls and floor. Where some hotels fall down is in stark, boring corridors and landings. Here they are all interestingly furnished with settees and antique wardrobes, spinning wheel, sewing machine, corn grader and old helmets.

The hotel is a Logis de France, Relais du Silence, a member of Châteaux Hotels Indépendents and Arc (Association des Rest-autrices Cuisinières – women chefs), for Mme Christine Moille is chef de cuisine while her husband handles the hotel. A winding road brings you to it from Beaune but it is well sign-posted.

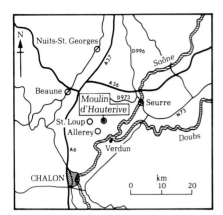

Beaune (15km) – get a good guide to Beaune and the wine roads. A superb medieval city with a bustling modern life. Don't miss Hôtel-Dieu, a hospital founded in 1443 by the Royal chancellor Nicolas Rolin for the poor and used until 1971, when a new building took over. 'It is fitting,' said Louis XI of Rolin, 'that he who made so many destitute in his life should build them an almshouse before he died.' It is still an old people's home. The street entrance looks rather dull but from the courtyard the building is gorgeous, a blaze of colour on the steep-pitched roof covered with glazed tiles in patterns and with a double-row of gables. There is an open gallery all round. See inside the Grand'Salle, or Paupers' Ward, 235 feet (72 metres) long, with a row of fourteen four-poster beds on each side placed so all the sick could see and follow the service in the chapel. In the museum is a magnificent 1443 polyptych of the Last Judgement by Rogier van de Weydens – an altarpiece shown to the sick and dying on special occasions as a warning if they did not repent. It has been compared with Jan van Eyck's altarpiece of the Lamb of Ghent.

Rolin left vineyards to the hospital so that the wine could be sold to meet expenses, and more were left later by repenting sinners, so that now the Hospice owns thirty vineyards in Beaune, Corton, Meursault, Vergeless, Savigny, Pommard, Volnay, Monthelie, Auxey-Duresses. The wines are sold at a trade-only auction in November, drawing buyers from all over the world. With the determination of an All Black rugby forward, you might get into the Hospice cellars to taste the wine the night before. It is a terrible scrum. Better to taste the young Beaujolais that night in the town hall. Two other things not to miss in Beaune are the group of tapestries from Middle Ages to Renaissance in the Collegiale Notre Dame, 'La Vie de la Vierge' (Life of the Virgin), and the wine museum in the old house of the Dukes of Burgundy, with some superb old glasses as well as old pressoirs, and magnificent modern tapestries by Jean Lurçat and Michel Tourlière.

To drive close to the most well-known wine villages take N74 northward from Beaune, then on to D122 just after Vougeot up to Dijon. South from Beaune, take D973 to Auxey-Duresses, left through Meursault to join N74 to Chagny, then D981 to Givry, through the Côte Chalonaise. Take a temperate driver – tastings abound. They are trying to sell you wine.

If tasting wine to buy don't eat cheese cheese can make Ordinaire taste like a Grand Cru.

Christiane Moille is a thoughtful and careful chef and is not content to stand still. She takes regular courses in the kitchens of famous chefs to pick up new ideas and improve her technique.

Her tourist menu is good value, her gastronomic menu has quality, interest and choice. Among the starters in the gastronomic menu was one of her specialities, her own fresh foie gras of duck, but I chose oeufs brouillés aux truffes et à la fondue de tomate. It is wonderful what morsels of truffles can do to scrambled eggs. Then I had her very special dish – turbot à la feuille de choux et à la moelle. A most unusual dish of turbot cooked in blanched white cabbage leaves and slices of beef marrow in a bain-marie in the oven. One magazine called it a sort of fish pot au feu. It is very tasty.

For main course I chose emincée de filet de Charolais à la caillette de brebis et pomme de terre en robe du champ – a description almost worthy of an American menu. It was thinly-sliced fillet steak of Charolais served with a sausage of sheep's liver and offal with herbs and baked potatoes in their jackets. Barbara thought that the veal kidneys roasted with shallots and served with noodles were delicious, too. Beware – pâtes fraîches are noodles, not pâté. On the cheese course we chose salade au bresse bleu, and this blue cheese, though factory made, is much nicer when it has not had long journeys in lorries and been in a fridge store.

Burgundy has some splendid cheeses. I have mentioned some of the good local cheeses in my entry on Moulin des Pommerats at Venizy, St Florentin, (page 113). A goat's cheese worth trying is Chevrotton de Macon, also known as Cabrion or Maconnais — cone-shaped, eaten either fresh when white and creamy, or aged and stronger. Some farms use mixed goat's and cow's milk. Mme Moille makes a good varied fresh fruit salad of the season covered in strawberry sauce.

The wine list has a choice of fourteen lovely white Burgundies, twenty-six red Burgundies, seven Côtes de Beaujolais and one cheap Côtes de Provence red.

If you are celebrating, try the inevitably-pricey 1979 white, dry, rich Corton-Charlemagne, a wine so good that it often fetches a higher price at sales than any red Burgundy. Some small producers sell only direct to private customers.

There is also an excellent 1982 *premier cru* Chablis from Philippe Testut, one of the best producers, but if you have not drunk it before, try the Rully of Jean-François Delorme. He has done much to improve Rully wines, bringing out the fruity taste. The whites are clean and fresh on the tongue and should be drunk fairly young — up to four years. The red wines, even from Delorme, do not impress me so much although I have heard a top British importer call them 'charming and attractive'. Most sparkling Burgundy made by the Champagne method comes from Rully, although you rarely find the name on the label.

Among the cheaper reds I would try Givry, also from Delorme. This wine was once very popular, rating alongside Beaune and Volnay. It is improving again, and goes well with red meats and heavy, flavoursome sauces. It has a dry, sharp, back-of-the-tongue taste, combined with fruitiness. There are some mouthwatering dearer and greater reds from some of the best vignerons. I would certainly enjoy a Pernand Vergelenes Côte de Beaune 1973 from Dubreuil-Fontaine or the Aloxe-Corton 1981 from Moroni, both at fair prices for Burgundy. Let us face it, Burgundy prices have become grossly inflated, thanks mostly to buying by the Americans and the Japanese, although the French also blame the British for the high auction prices. Bordeaux wines have not suffered so much from this inflation. Cheapest wines on this list are a Brouilly from Côte de Beaujolais, a nice fruity satisfying wine, and a cheap Moulin à Vent, deep coloured, a lot of guts, and velvety texture. You can be fooled by Moulin into drinking too much.

Hostellerie du Moulin des Pommerats

**Le Moulin des Pommerats
Venizy, (4km SE St Florentin
by N77 road to Chablis –
20km), 89210 Brienon-sur-
Armençon, Yonne.
Telephone: (86) 35.08.04.
Rooms D–G (some in annexe
20 yds away);
menus A, B, C, D;
half-board D.
Closed February, school
holidays, Sunday evenings,
Mondays low season. Rooms
held until 5p.m., after which
telephone to confirm.
Visa, Euro, Diners.**

An intimate and lovable little hideaway. A beautiful old white mill with a red roof in a pretty garden of flowers and trees alongside the little river Créanton, which is jumping with trout; comfortable, very friendly and reasonable.

The patron-chef, Paul Remaux d'Equainville understands the British, even the awkward ones. He fought as an RAF officer from 1940–45. His little hotel is a member of Châteaux Hôtels Indépendents, often less luxurious, a bit cheaper and cosier than the impressive Relais et Châteaux Hôtels, but as good in their own way.

The very-adjacent annexe, as old as the mill, has one jumbo-size bedroom with beams, large wooden bed and wardrobe, settee, armchair, TV, plenty of tables and lamps. The large bathroom has two basins. The other bedrooms are certainly not cramped.

One problem with smaller French hotels is the lack of sitting space except in foyer and bedrooms. Here there is a large comfortable lounge with open fire, a smaller 'English' room with English hunting scenes and a little bar, put in for the British and the patron himself, who likes British bars.

Green window boxes with flowers outside most windows give a charming effect. At St Florentin (4km) is tennis, horse riding, swimming pool and fishing at a fish farm. St Florentin makes a famous and powerful cheese.

Food & Drink

The cooking is traditional straightforward Burgundy cooking with good fresh meat and fish and a choice of fresh vegetables. The menus are good value with one absolute-bargain three-course weekday meal, and both the card and the wines are most reasonably priced compared with many hotels of this quality.

The cheap menu offers an assortment of crudités (raw vegetables and peppers with a dip) or a good home-made country pâté, half a chicken or a grilled pork chop or dish of the day, with vegetables, and cheese or

LOCAL DRIVES

Chablis (20km): the golden gate to Burgundy wine, a nice little village with a charming walk under ancient trees beside the river. A good Grand Cru Chablis is possibly my favourite white wine. It is different from any other white Burgundy, uncompromisingly dry and just acidic enough to bring out the full flavour, which develops for three or four years. Only in good years will the top Grand Cru vineyards sell wine under their own names. In other years the wine is 'downgraded' to Premier Cru. From the main square of Chablis, across the river, you can actually see seven Grand Cru vineyards.

Tonnerre (26km) is an old town surrounded by vineyards and meadows and deals in wine.

Beyond Tonnerre are two celebrated Renaissance châteaux. Tanlay (8km E of Tonnerre), was started in 1559 by one of the Coligny brothers, Protestant leaders in the Wars of Religion. It is a beautiful rambling château with a moat, arcaded courtyard, a round tower topped by a Byzantine-looking lanterned dome and frescoes. (Visits Palm Sunday to 1 November except Mondays).

Ancy-le-Franc is a classical château rebuilt in 1546 in the new style just imported from Italy. The architect was the consultant-architect for Fontainebleau (visits Easter-All Saints' Day).

dessert. The middle-priced menu has five courses with a reasonable choice on each. But the dearest menu, with more choice, is very fairly priced and worth the extra.

Among starters were smoked salmon and foie gras purée, but we had one of the great cold dishes of Burgundy, jambon persillé de Bourgogne. The pig has an honoured place in Burgundian cooking, and mild cured hams of the mountains are splendid raw or cooked. For persillé, a whole ham is simmered with a pig's trotter in white wine, then shredded with a fork so that lean and fat are mixed. Successive layers of ham and chopped parsley are put in a bowl, the wine and ham stock poured over it, and it is left to set to a jelly, making a sort of super galantine. There were snails on the second course but we went for gambas (large prawns flambéed in Marc de Bourgogne, the spirit distilled from grape residue of skin, pips and stalk after wine-pressing. These were delicious.

I was particularly recommended to try Paul's lamb or his grilled fillet steak from this homeland of the white Charolais cattle, which the French believe produce the best beef in the world. I chose instead cailles aux airelles, two quails in a bilberry sauce. Quail can be very dry and hard. This was soft and succulent, and served with young haricots verts and salsifis, the long white delicately-flavoured root vegetable which looks rather like a big white carrot.

The cheeseboard is a speciality of this hotel, not only for variety, but for superb regional cheeses. St Florentin, a triple-cream cheese with a spicey smell and flavour, soft white inside, yellow outside; Chaource, a softer, smooth Camembert-like cheese from the Burgundy-Champagne borders; Soumaintrin, the Burgundy favourite, soft, yellow, with a crusty golden rind and strong flavour; Vézelay, the local goats' milk cheese; Epoisses, small round, soft cow's milk cheese.

Choice of desserts is good, including mystère (ice cream in meringue coated with nuts flambéed in Grand Marnier – superb), dame blanche (peach poached, served cold with ice cream, pineapple and whipped cream), and omelette Norvégienne (sponge filled with ice cream, covered in meringue and served hot).

The wine list is outstandingly good value, with a very sensible choice of red Burgundies, from a simple Beaujolais to an Hospices de Beaune at a fair price for such luxury. He has an outstanding supplier of Yonne wines, Simonnet-Febvre from just outside Chablis. A lesser-known red you might like to try with quail, lamb or cheese is their Bourgogne Irancy. Sometimes called 'red Chablis', it is a little acid at first, but softens in bottle to a pleasant, quite cheap drink. If you cannot manage a bottle on your own or just want to taste it Paul serves a half-litre pichet, as he does with several cheaper wines, including the ordinary Chablis.

For a more expensive red, I would choose the Gevrey Chambertin.

For white, do try Chablis Premier Cru Montée de Tonnerre from Simonnet-Febvre – one of the best I have ever had. I have drunk it when possible for years. Chablis has suffered greatly from bottlers labelling other wine as Chablis; American wine Chablis simply isn't Chablis, and is rubbish beside the real thing. Buy Chablis bottled in Chablis. Words on labels like 'Domaine bottled' mean nothing. The Domaine might be in Normandy or Provence.

Champagne is much cheaper here than in many hotels.

Paul also serves a traditional Kir as an aperitif – made with good double Crème de Cassis and an Aligoté white Burgundy, just like Canon Felix Kir, priest, Resistance leader and Mayor of Dijon, made it. There is no real substitute.

You can take home 10 bottles of wine from France.
Make it Chablis.
Paul will direct you to his famous suppliers just outside Chablis village.

Ostellerie du Vieux Pérouges
place du Tilleul, 01800
Pérouges, Ain (just off N84
Lyon-Geneva road, 34km NW
Lyon, 38km S of Bourg-en-
Bresse).
Telephone: (74) 61.00.88.
Rooms (some in ancient
Manoir across the square) G,
H;
menus B–E.
Closed Wednesday, Thursday
lunch except July, August.
Visa.

A masterpiece. A thirteenth-century house with latticework of timbers, in a medieval hilltop village, and a fifteenth-century manor house across the square, all surrounded by beautiful old buildings. No wonder this hostellerie is an official historic monument.

Pérouges has been preserved almost exactly as it was in medieval times (apart, blessedly, from drainage and plumbing), complete with cobbled streets, two original gateways and a double line of ramparts. It is a joy to walk around it.

A prosperous, free village of craftsmen over centuries, it fell on hard times when factories stole its customers and road and railway by-passed its narrow streets. From 1,500 people its population fell to eighty. In 1909, Anthelme Thibaut interested Edouard Herriot in saving it. Herriot was Radical Socialist Mayor of Lyon from 1905–55, Premier of France, and the man who made modern Lyon. The committee of Old Pérouges was formed, with artists, historians and well

known people. Old houses were repaired. Craftsmen returned to work there. Now inevitably it is used as a setting for historical films. So you can forgive it for playing to the tourist gallery a little.

Rooms in the Ostellerie are large and superbly furnished with antiques. Our room in the Manoir, called Chambre du Tambour (drum), had a large antique four-poster bed, a huge chest of drawers and an antique armchair covered in red and green stripes to match the bed cover and the curtains round the bed and across the windows. The ceiling was beamed. The bathroom (not thirteenth-century) had marble floor and walls. There were views from the windows over the rooftops. There are more rooms in two other houses round the square.

The dining room has a huge old open fireplace in stone. The inn has a fine collection of pewter – and a *Michelin* star for cuisine. And all this is run by Georges Thibaut, with his son Christophe as chef. I don't know where Pérouges would

LOCAL DRIVES

Lyon (34km) – the second largest urban area to Paris in France, with all that goes with that – industries, a university (famous for medicine), old buildings, theatres and museums – almost as many as London, museums devoted to the history of cloth, of hospitals and medicine, of marionettes and, more sadly, a museum of Resistance and Deportation, including memories of the great Lyon Resistance hero Jean Moulin.

Northwards on D433 is a super car museum ('Henri Malatre') with some magnificent early De Dion-Bouton, Bollée, Panhard-Levasser, Renault, Delahaye and dozens more; bikes and motorbikes, too.

Île Crémieu (24km S to Crémieu town) is a little-known area of cliffs, caves, lakes, rock outcrops in the fields, farms with stone roofs and country houses (gentilhommières). A circuit (56km) could be: D52 from Crémieu past lakes to Charette, then D52C to Ambérieu. 2km on right are Grottes de la Balme, caves with many big chambers, underground rivers, waterfalls and lake. The visit takes 1½ hours. Back on the D65, then left to Hières, take the D52A through Gorges d'Amby beside river to Châtelans. See the plateau de Larins to the right, then take the D521 to Annoisin Châtelans and the D52 to Crémieu, where there is a pleasant walk through the old town.

be without the Thibaut family. Georges's father was Mayor of Pérouges for years, the main shop is in the family, and even the guidebook was written by one of them.

Food & Drink

Crayfish, trout and pike fresh from local rivers, cheeses from the Savoy, Dauphiné and Burgundy, milk and maize-fattened free-range chickens of Bresse, mushrooms from Bugey – no wonder Christophe Thibaut likes to use regional ingredients in traditional local recipes. He cooks with more lightness of touch than chefs of the mountains beyond Pérouges. His *Michelin* star is earned in an area of fierce culinary competition around Lyon.

You eat from copper dishes on old tables beneath an old tapestry, served by waitresses in traditional old costume and lace caps, and your medieval

aperitif is served in a pewter goblet.

There are six suggested menus, but you can juggle with the choices from one menu to another. All include, between cheese and dessert, galette Pérougienne, a round flat cake (rather stodgy) served with cream. It comes with breakfast, too.

The temptation is to go for Bresse chicken on two courses. The chicken-liver pâté, gâteau de foies de volaille, is delicious, but so are the crayfish. I suggest the truite en gelée – a delightful dish of cold trout which is cooked in a court-bouillon with white wine, the liquid reduced, gelatine added, the fish glazed with it and put in the fridge. I was glad to see the recipe in Shirley Conran's *Cookbook* – we don't often have cold trout in Britain.

I would certainly have the Bresse chicken, which is in a different world from any chicken I have had since Surrey Capon seemingly became extinct with our entry into Europe. Have gratin Dauphinois with it – those superb potatoes baked in cream.

A salad with nut oil is served after the main course. The good cheeseboard included Barbara's favourite soft cream cheese with walnuts in it, also the Bresse cheeses – Bleu de Bresse and mild fruity Bressan goat's milk cheese. After that galette, fruit, or a choice of many home-made sorbets are served.

The medieval aperitif is Ypocras, called Hypocras elsewhere. It is a 'stimulant et digestif de première ordre' and called 'Bon pour la santé', and

is made to the veritable recipe of Guillaume Tirel Taillevent, head cook to Phillippe VI of Valois and Charles VI of France and author of one of the earliest cookbooks. The drink is red wine heated with honey and herbs, then cooled.

Apart from the wonderful wines of Burgundy and Beaujolais, both within range of Pérouges and well represented on the wine list, there are some pleasant regional wines around here.

Savoie wines have achieved appellation contrôlée status but Bugey wines to the west are still VDQS. The Savoie whites made from the Jacquère grape are acidic and weak in alcohol; those made from the Roussette grape are stronger and have more flavour. There is a good one on this list, but the best white is the Roussette-du-Bugey Montagnieu of Jean Peillot, one of the best whites of the whole area. There is a fair, and fairly-cheap, Bugey Gamay red on the list, but I would pay a little more for a Fleurie or Brouilly Beaujolais. A Fleurie goes very nicely with the delicate flavour of Bresse chicken. When Burgundies or Beaujolais are within hailing distance it is difficult to ignore them – if the price is right.

To avoid high-season day-trippers in this mediaeval village, make for the unknown – Ile Crémieu

SOUTH AND SOUTH EAST

AUBERGE ★★★ DE LA FENIERE

Auberge de la Fenière
Route N453, Raphèle-en-
Provence, 13200 Arles (5km E
from Arles on N453 north of
the big N113).
Telephone: (90) 98.47.44.
Rooms D–G; apartments for
3–4 people G;
menus B, C.
Hotel open all year;
restaurant
closed 1 November to 20
December, and Saturday.
Dinner only Easter to 1
November.
Visa, Euro, Amex, Diners.

Arles is a magic city, a place for all seasons and many interests. But after a day slogging its narrow streets up steep slopes, hunting for parking spots and coping with jams, what a delight it is to find a Relais du Silence standing alone among fields and trees just 5km away.

Auberge de la Fenière, covered in creeper and surrounded by flowers in a beautifully-kept garden, was converted from a farmhouse by the patron Belzunce Legros and his wife nineteen years ago when they returned from Morocco. It is a really pretty place, with sympathetic and helpful owners.

Inside, the Moroccan influence shows a little with a typical Moroccan carpet on the wall of the lounge bar, and the old farmhouse shows in the beamed ceilings and the old stone oven next to the stone open fireplace in the dining room. The attractive iron lamps were made by M. Legros himself. He did much of the conversion with his own hands, too, a few rooms at a time over the years.

The furnishings are heavy Provençal style, with thick wood and flowered wallpapers in the bedrooms, giving it a solid, warm and permanent look. A true haven, it seduces you. The longer you stay, the more you like it.

Arles is dominated by its Roman arena, the huge building seems to meet you wherever you turn. Built when Julius Caesar moved the Roman capital of Provence from Marseilles to Arles around 46 BC, it held 27,000 spectators, but its third tier is now missing. Bull fights are held there. Operas and plays are given in what remains of the Roman theatre.

In St Trophime's church, once a cathedral, Barbarossa, Holy Roman Emperor, was crowned King of Arles in the twelfth century and good King René married Jeanne de Laval. Earlier St Augustine was consecrated first Bishop of Canterbury there. It has an interesting mixture of styles, outside and inside, a fourth-century sarcophagus, seventeenth- to eighteenth-century Flemish paintings, tapestries and ivories. The twelfth-century cloisters,

Beaucaire and Tarascon (20km N of Arles) have scowled at each other across the Rhône for 700 years, though now joined by a bridge. Once this was the boundary between France and the Holy Roman Empire. Beaucaire is now industrial; its eleventh-century castle, much dismantled by order of Richelieu, is now a shell, though chapel, towers and walls remain. From the thirteenth century until railways came, Beaucaire was the site of a great annual fair which 300,000 people attended. The riverside quays remain, still dealing in wine. Tarascon, where St Marthe tamed the monster called Tarasque, still has King René's fifteenth-century castle – rugged, strong yet beautiful, with a moat on three sides and a sheer drop of 120 feet to the Rhône on the other. It is a treasure, with its parade ground where armoured soldiers drilled, banqueting hall with huge open fireplace, chapel, royal apartments all remarkably intact. The reason is that for centuries until 1926 it was a prison. In the eighteenth century POWs – mostly sailors from the ships Zephyr and Constantine taken off Toulon in the Seven Years War – were imprisoned here and their graffiti is still on the walls, some in rhyme.

The Camargue (220 squares miles of Rhône delta marshes) starts at Arles, though the first part you meet has been drained, desalinated and cultivated since 1941 with rice, wheat, vines and fruit, and even has trees planted. You can still see the little black bulls, bred for bullfights in which they are not killed but have rosettes tipped off their horns; quick-footed creamy white horses and Camargue cowboys in large felt hats look after them. Take N570 from Arles to Mas du Pont du Rousty, a sheep farm now housing the Camargue Museum. There's another information centre further on at Ginès, a bird sanctuary open until sunset at Pont du Gau, a museum open 1 April to 1 October at Boumian with wax tableaux showing the life of a cowboy here and a gypsy encampment.

The road is lined from Albaron with restaurants, hotels and 'ranches' in Camargue style, offering conducted horse rides. At Stes Maries-de-la-Mer, where gypsies gather three times a year for pilgrimages and fairs, is a fortified church associated with a legend of Mary Magdalene and Martha.

A mile away along D38 you can take a boat (one per day, late afternoon, 1½ hours) on the Petit Rhône to the grazing pastures of the bulls and horses – a good chance of seeing wild birds such as grey heron, osprey, duck and flamingoes. The road round Vacarès Lake from Stes Maries skirts the Camargue National Reserve. Pink flamingoes are here in summer, teal in winter, and hundreds of thousands of migrants from swallows to purple herons and osprey pass through in spring and autumn.

carved with scenes from the Bible and Provençal legend, are serenely lovely. Of many museums, I like Musée Réattu in the graceful former priory of the Knights of St John. The tapestries are gorgeous; they include seventeenth-century Brussels tapestries, a wonderful tapestry and a roomful of ceramics by the great modern artist Jean Lurçat, and a powerful work of the modern Spaniard Grau Garriga; also coloured sketches by Picasso, and works by Léger, Gauguin, Vlaminck and Rouault, and sculptures by Bourdelle.

Montmajour Abbey (7km N of Arles by N570, D17) is a tenth-century fortified Benedictine Abbey with beautiful carved cloisters and a wild history. The self-indulgent monks sacked it when thrown out by the Order; after the scandal of its Commandary abbot, Cardinal de Rohan, Queen Marie-Antoinette and a necklace, Louis XVI suppressed the abbey; then antique and property dealers bought it and started selling it off in bits. Much restored now, it is open on Tuesdays and Wednesdays. Climb 124 steps up the tower and, given luck with the weather, you can see Arles, the Cevennes, Crau Plain and the Alpilles. On the road between the Abbey and Fontvieille is Alphonse Daudet's windmill (*Lettres de Mon Moulin*), now a museum with an interesting *table d'orientation* showing the directions of the thirty-two winds which blow over Provence.

Food & Drink

Catherine Legros believes in giving her guests plenty of choice on each course in her two menus, even if that does mean putting a small supplement on a few dishes. She is a member of Arc, the exclusive association of women chefs, and cooks delightfully in a classic way.

Her specialities include tender chicken grilled with Provence herbs and flambéed with brandy. It was served with vegetable fennel. Barbara said it was one of the finest grilled chickens she had tasted. I like her estouffade of beef – a simple enough dish of beef stewed very slowly in a tightly closed pot with wine, herbs, tomatoes, vegetables and beans. Served with local rice, it is a speciality of the Camargue, probably originally because those fighting black bulls are not killed in the ring or even injured, and can live a long time, hence the slow cooking. Since the paddy-fields reached the Camargue in the 1940s to fill wartime stomachs, rice has become part of local cookery.

If you like squid, which I would never order but would eat if served to me, les encornets à l'Armoricaine have been recommended to me – sautéed in oil with white wine, brandy, garlic, shallots and tomatoes, and served with the rice.

On the cheaper menu you start with the soup of the day, and Madame is known for her splendid home stockpot soups. Out of ten choices for entrée, my choice would be Arles sausage. I even like the supermarket version of this spicey,

garlicked rough-chopped sausage of dried pork which I prefer to drier salami, and bring it home every journey.

Among desserts is another of Madame's specialities of which she is justly proud – tartelettes chaudes (little hot tarts filled with fruit). Apple tarts are the favourites. Téton au chocolat is pretty good, too. It is a type of local peach called 'angel's breasts' with a hot chocolate sauce, and you must order it at the start of the meal so that the sauce is fresh and perfect.

Though the dearer menu has such delicacies as foie gras of duck, smoked salmon, Madame's speciality of roulades de saumon à la crème, and a lovely salmon trout flambéed in pastis among its choices, I think the cheaper menu is very good value.

There was little on the card which was not on one menu or both except asparagus.

There are some well-chosen Provence wines on the list, as well as a very drinkable house red and a small selection of the wines of the main areas of France at reasonable prices. There is a good Cassis Blanc de Blancs, another good value white from Rousset, east of Aix-en-Provence, called Château de la Bégude, which you are unlikely to find in a supermarket because it nearly

all goes to regular customers. One of the best red wines of Bandol, aged in the wood for eighteen months, rich and strong, is here – Moulin des Costes, plus its white and rosé. But if you have not tried a Palette (and that is probable, because it is one of the smallest appellations in France), then do try the best of them – Château Simone. Among the grapes used in the blend are some of the old Provence varieties which disappeared from most vineyards in the modernization of vine-growing and wine-making in the 1950s. The red is aged in the wood and has quality and a unique flavour, and I think you will be surprised, too, by the quality and individuality of the white, which is also on the list.

They certainly go very well with Madame's classic Provence cooking.

In Basque country, l'enniére was straw kept between ground-floor animals and people sleeping above. Heat from the animals kept the straw and people warm without manure smells getting through – fine air – fennière.

**Hôtel Le Calalou
Moissac Bellevue, 83630
Aups, Var (driving from
North, take D85 from Digne,
then D907 to Riez, then D11,
D13, left on D30 to Moissac).
Telephone: (94) 70.03.16.
Rooms F, G;
menus A, B;
half-board E.
Closed mid-December to mid-
March; Mondays low season.
Euro, Amex.**

*You need at least two days
to explore this wild land. A
week would fly past.*

Wild country, close to some of
the last wilderness of Western
Europe, Les Gorges du Verdon.
Le Calalou is a bright, comfortable and attractively-sited
haven from which to explore
the harsh natural sculptures of
Verdon and the big man-made
lake of Sainte-Croix. Barbara
says she could lie all day by the
hotel swimming pool just
looking at the view.

The house looks like a big old
Provençal farm. In fact, it was
built ten years ago by the
architect-husband of Madame
Armande Vernet, la patronne.
The Vernets come from the gorgeous French Caribbean island
of Martinique. Her mother does
the cooking, which has a few
Créole dishes.

The attractive bright dining
room, with white garden chairs
and tables and orange cloths
and awning, has sliding glass
doors to the terrace, around
which are beds of vivid flowers
and old olive trees which
heighten the farm effect. There
is a cosy indoor restaurant for
winter.

Inside, the hotel is light and
bright, with Provençal-style

furniture which I like a lot,
brightly-coloured cushions
and modern light bedrooms,
with plenty of cupboard space
and nice bathrooms.

There is good fishing, sailing,
water-skiing and wind-surfing
on Lake Sainte-Croix.

Food & Drink

Le Calalou is a cooking dish
(which is what paëlla means,
too), and the Calalou served
here is a Martinique dish like a
paëlla but with smoked fish,
smoked meats and sausage. It is
on the card with three other
specialities of the cook from
Martinique, Mme Léonil. The
others are poulet Créole
(chicken with rice, peppers, tomatoes and spices), colombo
Martiniquais, which I have not
tried, but is hand-reared pigeon ('dove'), with pineapple
and almost certainly rum used
in the preparation, and a couscous which Barbara had when
she tried the set meal given to
people on pension or half-
pension terms. Apart from not
wanting to fill up with too

Aups (7km): 2,000 feet (610 metres) up, with ramparts, a ruined castle, narrow streets and a big main square with magnificent plane trees and several fountains: very photogenic. It is known for honey from bees which feed off the huge lavender fields up in the Moustiers and Verdon gorges and the wild flowers of this country where fields are ablaze with poppies – weedkillers are not used round here. The lavender is in bloom in July. The Simon Segal museum in a former convent chapel in Aups has 300 modern paintings.

Take D77 from Aups to Tourtour (10km), a medieval hill village with two ruined castles and aerial views. On D51 left, another 8km, is Ampus, a very pretty village. Continue to Châteaudouble, with a deep green gorge of the river Nartuby. Follow this on D955 to Draguignan, a town with medieval houses, gates and fountains and nineteenth-century straight boulevards and walks laid out by Baron Haussmann, who did the same for Paris. It's a wine-producing district, with a huge market on Saturday mornings. In August 1944, 10,000 British and American soldiers landed around here by parachute or glider and joined with the Maquis to free the area.

Grand Canyon du Verdon: an incredibly dramatic gorge cut through rock by the river Verdon, with gorges 20 to 320 feet (6 to 100 metres) wide and cliffs up to 5000 feet (1523 metres) deep. It is magnificent

and almost frightening. Only experienced hill and rock scramblers could approach the gorge until 1947, when the Corniche Sublime was cut through rock on the south side. In 1973 Route des Crêtes (Crest road) on the north bank was completed. Now there are virtually two circuits to be driven to see the gorge properly. Take your time. There are many viewing points and it is worth stopping at them.

From Moissac-Bellevue take D9 (10km) to the man-made Lac de Ste Croix, then right fork to Moustiers Ste Marie, a town in a most dramatic and beautiful setting. It is built half-way up a rock face on either side of a deep gorge, through which water cascades from a breach in the rock above the village. The two halves are joined by a narrow bridge. Across the gorge a massive gold star is strung on a chain. In 1249 the local lord, taken prisoner in the Crusades, vowed that if he got home safely he would hang a star of Bethlehem across the gorge for all to see. His star lasted 600 years before it was blown down in a storm, but a new one replaced it. The once-great blue-patterned Moustiers crockery has been made here since 1680, but it is not what it was. There is a museum of the old Clerissy blue-patterned crockery. You can join the Crest road at La Palud where there is a restaurant.

Sillans-la-Cascade (9km SW Aups on D22) is an attractive fortified village on river bank with signposted path through woods to a waterfall with a 138-feet (41-metre) drop.

much rice or semolina, I was rather put off couscous when attending a high-powered lunch in a mosque given by the President of Tunisia. Passing by around 10a.m., I saw old ladies preparing the presidential couscous on a fire outside, in an old oil drum, and throwing the ingredients, including lamb and guts, into it straight from the dirty ground.

This Calalou couscous was perfectly wholesome but unusual. Apart from lamb and vegetables, it had in it chick peas, spices, merguez sausage, and meat balls. Barbara then had a delicious triple creamy Brillat cheese, which came from Normandy but is now made all over France. Then apple tart.

The cheap menu has a choice of three dishes on the two main courses, but the dearer menu, which is good value, had a very good civet de porcelet when we were there, a rich stew of piglet cooked in wine, as one choice

of four on the main course. Crudités (raw vegetables) with sauce dips were served first, then a choice of goose liver galantine, raw ham or trout meunière.

The second night we ate from the card. The dishes were straightforward home cooking. Pleasant, but not gastronomic, although this, like Périgueaux and the Dordogne, is truffle country, and there was a brouillade aux truffes (truffles with scrambled egg), a truffled duck foie gras, and a cou de canard farci truffe – duck's neck stuffed with sausage, duck liver and chopped truffles

and cooked in duck fat. It comes out like a sausage. It is one of those peasant dishes, invented to fill empty stomachs, which have become gourmets' delights. It was said in the Périgord that if you have the neck of a goose, a loaf of bread and a bottle of wine you can ask your friends to a feast.

The wine list is fairly short but very adequate, with prices reasonable. Three cheap wines and one slightly dearer, all Cabernet Sauvignon wine, from nearby Villecroze, and a cheap red comes from a good area for red wine, Pierrefeu. It is called Domaine de Kennel.

Most of the other Provence wines come from leading producers and are dearer. For the white I would choose the heavyish, strong Domaine Paternal from Cassis mentioned in the Mas d'Entremont entry (page 145). The Ott Côtes de Provence Blanc de Blancs is too dear. There is a perfectly drinkable Chablis on the list at half the price. For my red I would choose the excellent Moulin des Costes Bandol, reasonably priced, or the very reasonably priced St Emilion Château Haut-Badon.

A peaceful and beautiful spot to drink wine and dream.

Les Deux Rocs
Seillans, 83440 Var (in
Montagne de Malay 6km W of
Fayence; 31km from Grasse
off Grasse-Draguignan road
D562).
Telephone: (94) 76.05.33
Rooms C–F;
menus A, B, C;
half-board D–F.
Closed 3 November to mid-
March; restaurant closed
Tuesdays.

An elegant eighteenth-century house beside a memorial fountain in a little square, with tables under the trees around the terrace. This is the 'new' part of Seillans, just outside the medieval walls. The local people fled up here in the Middle Ages to defend themselves against the Saracens, and built their houses together facing inwards so that their walls (four-feet (1½ metres) thick) formed the walls of the town. Some of them, in cream stone, still stand four or five storeys high among old gateways, a ruined twelfth-century château with keep, narrow paved streets and fountains. The town falls down a hillside.

The old house is charmingly furnished, each of the bedrooms quite different but all cheerful, with attractive prints and excellent bathrooms. The dining room is heavily beamed. It has a delightful ambience, and many people, including Britons, return annually. La patronne, Lise Hirsch, was a biochemist in Paris.

Seillans has for some years been something of an artists' and writers' colony. Max Ernst lived and painted here. There are several local craftsmen working in the village – potters, craftsmen in iron and olive wood, and weavers. Perfume is made, too.

The views from the village to the Esteral hills are superb and the old roads, walls and archways so photogenic that in season you can fall over amateur photographers. The name Seillans came from *seilhanso*, the Provençal word for pots of boiling oil used to discourage Saracens from climbing the walls.

Just outside the village is the chapel of Notre Dame de l'Ormeau, with a statue of the Virgin, believed in the Middle Ages to be miracle-working. It was buried to save it from the Saracens and discovered by a ploughman 200 years later. More exciting artistically are the sculptures of an unknown Italian monk. He arrived in the village as a refugee in 1350, and on finding that he was a pupil of the great Nicolas Pisano the Seigneur of Seillans said he could stay providing he decor-

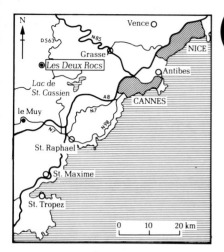

Gorge of Verdon, though it's hardly local. It starts about 70km away, but is one of the most spectacular and lovely sights in France. Drive to Draguignan westwards, take D955 N to Comps sur Artuby, then left on D71 to the Corniche Sublime. (For more on Gorges du Verdon, see the entry under Le Calalou, Moissac Bellevue, page 124).

Grasse (31km) is a tourist cliché and crowded, but don't miss it. It has held world supremacy in perfume making since the eighteenth century and you can visit the factories. See, too, the interesting old part of the town, the villa of the eighteenth-century painter Jean-Honoré Fragonard, now a museum, and the twelfth-century cathedral with an attached museum of Admiral de Grasse who was largely responsible for our defeat in the American War of Independence. He blockaded the British Army at Yorktown, compelling it to surrender. Later he was beaten by Rodney and taken prisoner to London, where he was fêted! (This museum is due to move to another part of Grasse.)

St Raphaël (41km) – summer and winter sea resort with old harbour still used for fishing, crowded in high season, good little fish restaurants.

Elegant and intimate. The two real rocks are an outcrop in the square and rather ugly.

ated the apse. He took two years over his primitive masterpiece, sculpted on wood and vividly coloured.

Food & Drink

Patricia Sanchez, the young chef here, has been chided by a French guide for cooking traditionally – duck with peppers, lamb chop, trout in almonds. It depends how they are cooked, doesn't it? And how good and fresh the ingredients are. We think the meals here are very nicely cooked, and are very good value, which also matters to us.

There is a low-priced three-course weekday menu, with a reasonable choice. Two middle-priced menus at the same price were totally different. The first, which Barbara chose, was a 'menu minceur' (for slimmers) but she could hardly feel deprived after it. She chose a house salad, containing lettuce, grapefruit, apples, bean sprouts, tomatoes and peppers, then tranches de gigot, little thick slices of leg of lamb grilled on a spit with peppers, mushrooms, onions and tomatoes. Then she had cheese (a well-kept Brie and an excellent soft fromage blanc aux herbes were among the choices) and orange mousse.

On my eating-man's menu I started with a delicious leek tart, though I was told that the fish soup was very good. Then I had confit of duck, which I can rarely resist even in midsummer, cheese, and gâteau which was filled with fresh peaches and cream from a good choice of pâtisserie. I thought the menu was excellent value. One choice for main dish was entrecôte Villette, a name I have not heard for many years. Villette is the suburb of Paris where the best meat in France was sold. Perhaps it still is.

On the card was a genuine Crottin de Chavignol, goat's milk cheese from Berry served grilled. Crottin means manure and this gorgeous sharp strong cheese is said by critics to smell like it. There are imposters on some menus – ordinary goat's cheese or Chavignol of Sancerre posing as Crottin.

The dearer menu and the card contained straightforward old favourites – nothing 'inventive', as the fashion has it. But we heard nothing but praise for the cuisine from French and Britons.

The wine list has an extremely cheap vin de Pays (Château de Meaulx), some cheap and very drinkable Côtes de Provence, including Pierrefeu Blanc de Blancs which we had with our starters, a red, for which Pierrefeu is better known, and Bagnis red (very good value), rosé and white from Estandon, (the red would go well with the fish soup or the lamb brochette). But I think the cooking deserves a better wine and for a bit more you can get one of the best wines of Provence, La Laidière red from Bandol.

For a refreshing fizzy drink, try Perlant Imperial, white which is *petillant* – sparkling slightly. It can get too hot in midsummer for red wines at lunchtime, although the French seem to knock them back with little effect. The siesta is definitely recommended.

Hostellerie Bérard
La Cadière d'Azur, 83740 Var
(9km above Bandol, 5km from
N8 (Marseille-Toulon road)
and N559 (Marseille-Toulon
by the coast)).
Telephone: (94) 29.31.43
Rooms D–G (suite);
menus B, C, E;
half board E–G.
Closed mid-October to 30
November.
Visa.

'Get thee to a nunnery,' said Hamlet, and the one I would choose for cool in summer heat, to escape the crowds of the Côte d'Azur, for good food and charming ambience is Hostellerie Bérard.

Last time we retreated there it was so hot in the sunbowl of Bandol beach that even the sea seemed a bit overheated and I sat in a cold bath after lunch to work.

Two of the three buildings which make up this hotel were part of a convent. From the fourth century, this lovely village in the hills was called Cathedra, meaning place of refuge and repose. Despite a certain number of tourists who come from the coast resorts, especially in mid-summer, to see the old stone buildings with balconies, arched alleys and tree-shaded streets, La Cadière is still peaceful enough. Some of the shops are run by artisans and artists, such as the leather shop and the nearby pottery and weaving studio of Martine Kistner. The mill produces olive oil. The vineyards on the surrounding hills produce Bandol wines; that is why the village has prospered.

The old main building of the hotel has white, vaulted ceilings, red tiled floors and an attractive dining room with a log fire used in winter for spit-roasts; and a summer terrace, covered to protect you from the sun, with views over rooftops to the hills. Across an alley, another part of the convent has been beautifully converted into bedrooms with views over the heated swimming pool. The rooms are named after shrubs and plants. Ours was called 'Mustard'. A few yards down the road is another flowered terrace with a little bar and magnificent views for miles across the vine and olive-covered hills, alongside are more bedrooms. All the rooms are individually furnished, very comfortable, and have excellent modern bath or shower rooms. The service is smooth and professional, the sympathetic attention of the patronne, Danielle Bérard is delightful.

Food & Drink

René Bérard is a superb and inventive chef. He has some excellent dishes on his card, but they are dear. The menus are good and good value.

But if you don't mind paying what you might normally pay for a whole meal for one fish dish, one of his specialities is a delight. Called feuilleté de loup au Champagne, it is complicated to make and although M. Bérard very kindly told me the recipe, it is a bit long to pass on. Briefly, it is loup de mer (sea bass) gutted and boned, skinned, but with its head and tail left on, stuffed with chervil and button mushrooms. It is then wrapped in a thin coat of puff pastry, baked and served with a sauce of Champagne, slightly-sour cream, fish fumet, mussels and scallops.

The cheapest menu has four courses with fair choice. The second menu, which I had last time, is excellent value. First-course choices included fish terrine, asparagus in cream sauce, Parma ham, or the soup, which I chose. I am not normally a fish soup man but this soupe de poisson de roches, like a cross between a soup and a bouillabaisse, was very pleasing. Instead of moules sauce poulette – mussels in a thick creamy sauce – I went for brouillade Provençale (a sort of super ratatouille). Then I had a thick slab of boned and rolled shoulder of lamb grilled in Provence herbs. It was delicious. The cheeses were in perfect condition, the pâtisseries magnificent enough to tempt a fasting saint.

The Bérard cellars include a fine choice of local Bandol wines. Nearly all the best houses are represented, including Moulin de la Roque, La Cadière's own wine cooperative, with red, white and rosé, and the local Moulin des Costes wines of the Bunan brothers, whose Mas de la Rouvière on a hilltop near Le Castellet produces a rosé said by some to be the best in France, though I would challenge that.

The Bérard offers, too, the famous rosé and a red from

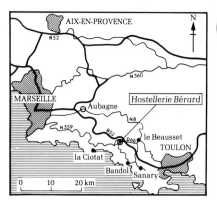

Bandol (9km) – an old-style seaside resort still loved by the French, with elegant palm-lined promenade, smart restaurants, a harbour where pleasure yachts now totally outnumber fishing boats, and sandy coves. Boats go to the isle of Bendor, deserted until 1955 when pastis-millionaire Paul Ricard made it an artistic centre for tourists with flowers and pines. You land at a fake Provençal fishing port, with a sailing club, and find, as you stroll around, three hotels, a village of potters, painters and jewellers, an excellent gallery of contemporary art, and a museum of wines and spirits, with fine glass and wines from fifty nations (closed Wednesdays). Sanary (3km SE of Bandol) is a less-sophisticated, and cheaper, fishing and yachting harbour, market; a jolly little place. Aldous Huxley once lived here. Offshore from Le Brusc, which has a pretty little port, is another Ricard isle, Embiez, now a seasport centre with marina, repair yard and an ocean research centre run by the marine biologist Alain Bombard (museum and aquarium).

On a hilltop near La Cadière is Le Castellet, a semi-deserted ancient village.

Château de Romassan at Le Castellet, part of the Ott family domaines. It was René Ott who, in 1930, bottled rosé in the attractive Greek-style bottle to attract restaurants and tourists to buy the under-estimated wine. The Ott blanc de blancs from their Clos Mireille vineyard is unusual and refreshing. It is made from Sémillon, the Sauternes grape, not the usual Chardonnay or Sauvignon.

For a rosé, I would pick Moulin des Costes. But the reds are the best of Bandol. Made from old-fashioned grapes (Ugni, Cinsault, Mourvedre, Grenache) they have to mature in the cask for at least eighteen months and have a lot of alcohol in them. They are smooth, too. Some cellars keep them in the cask for up to four years, but that makes them very dry. Better that after eighteen months they mature in bottle. Older red Bandol is a much underestimated wine. The Bérard has an excellent choice. The good wines are not cheap. I would go for the 1979 Domaine de la Laidière or a Domaine Templier (perhaps the best of Bandol reds). If you are in a real drinking mood you might be tempted by the label on the good Domaine de Frégate of Le Castellet. It is produced by M. Bernard de Pissy, president of the Bandol Syndicat des Vignerons.

Most caves offer tastings, including Moulin des Costes (La Cadière), Château de Romassan (Le Castellet) and Mas de la Rouvière (5–8p.m. Mondays, Tuesdays, Thursdays, Fridays).

Though cooler in summer than nearby sea resorts, La Cadière has the same winter climate as the resorts.

Hôtel Castel Anne
73 avenue Dr Valois, Voiron
38500, Isère (3km near La
Patinière on N92 Voiron to
Valence road; just off A48
Lyon-Grenoble motorway).
Telephone: (76) 05.86.00.
Rooms D–E;
menu A; card D, E.
Closed school holidays in
February; restaurant closed
Wednesdays.
Visa, Amex, Diners.

Those colour magazine advertisements of happy families lunching in their new sun lounge extension look rather pale once you have eaten in the dining room of Castel Anne. It is like a massive semi-circular domed greenhouse, big enough to swallow many modern bungalows. Tables on the ground floor look on to the well-kept lawns of the big garden and on a balcony with delicate iron railings; more tables have a longer view through their own huge windows. From the glass dome above hang baskets of flowers, and lampshades like big white balls. It has the stylish ostentation of the turn of the century, which is precisely when a rich local merchant added it to an older country house. It is in white stone and blends into the older building.

Jean-Yves Charvet and his wife used to live in New York, where he was chef at a restaurant, and they have added touches of American comfort to French flair in their bedrooms. They are in Empire-style with warm pinks, blues and greens, pretty but practical bathrooms, colour TV, radio and mini-bar. Some have doors to a big stone-balustraded balcony-terrace. It is a cosy, charming hotel.

This is not only a fine centre for exploring the Dauphiné mountains but a good hideout from the massive traffic problems of modern industrial Grenoble; also a good stopover hotel for motorists heading to or from the Riviera and wanting to avoid the A7 motorway.

Just outside Voiron is the distillery of the Chartreuse monastery where some of the few members of the Carthusian Order allowed to talk to the public distil the fragrant, strong yellow Chartreuse liqueur and the very strong green one. They use 130 different herbs, mostly collected on the mountainside or grown by the monks at the monastery higher up the mountain, distilled to a recipe given to the monks in 1605 as a health drink. It does my health a world of good. You can visit the distillery any day except winter Saturdays and Sundays.

The monastery of Chartreuse is 20km up the mountain, by N520 to St Laurent-du-Pont, then through the Gorge du Guiers Mort. You can visit La Correrie de la Grande Chartreuse, an annexe of the monastery used as an infirmary, guest house and place of protection for the fathers from breaking their vow of silence. Queen Victoria stayed there. It houses a Carthusian museum but you can no longer visit the monastery.

Grenoble (29km) has grown faster than any French city since 1945 and is complicated for drivers. It has some pleasant old quarters, including an early twelfth-century cathedral in the district where the writer Stendhal was born. Its art gallery includes old masters and a fine modern collection – Picasso, Utrillo, Matisse, Gauguin, Rouault. A téléphérique takes you to a terrace with superb city and mountain views. Uriage-les-Bains (10km past Grenoble on N524) is a charming spa in a mountain valley among trees.

Sassenage, just before Grenoble, is the gateway to Vercors Regional Park, magnificent mountain area and scene of a heroic stand by the French Resistance against the Nazi SS (see entry for Hôtel Les Oiseaux, Claix, page 148). There is a museum of the Resistance in Grenoble.

Chambéry and Lake Bourget (44km) – see entry under Hotel Ombremont, page 151.

Food & Drink

Jean-Yves Charvet's cooking is traditional and straight-forward, using as many regional ingredients as possible, and that is the way they like it here at the foot of the mountains. Lyon, 87km north, and Vienne are the places for the fancier, light dishes. His meals are also very good value.

The mountain pastures, forests and lakes of the Dauphiné and Savoie provide superb cream and cheese, good lake fish (including salmon from Lake Bourget near Chambéry), game and pork products, with many sausages. Jean-Yves uses them all in season, but he also serves a lot of sea fish which are brought very fast from the Atlantic to Lyon and then down the motorway. Gone are the days when you could only get fresh fish near the sea in France.

His cheap and only menu is good value. I was offered mackerel marinaded in white wine or a mixed green salad, which included wild leaves such as dandelion as well as lettuce and endive (salade de mesclun), with the super Jesus sausage of Morteau in the Jura (large, with a wooden pin for holding it when smoked over fir wood; made of pork liver). The main course was grilled lotte (monkfish) with aubergine purée or an excellent braised ham. Then cheese, and a choice of desserts.

This is a splendid area for cheeses. Many are on the Castel Anne board – Sassenage (semi-hard, blue veined cheese of cow's milk with a little goat's milk blended in), Tome de Savoie (cow's milk, light), Tome de chèvre (mountain farm goat's milk), St Marcellin (soft cream cheese of mixed cow's and goat's milk), and a very good fromage blanc (fresh, soft cream cheese).

Goat's milk cheese is used in the ravioles, served by Jean-Yves with fillet of sole and delightfully light and creamy. Ravioles are little puffs of leaf pastry filled with cheese – not to be confused with ravioli.

From the card I recommend as a starter his hot oysters gratin in season or his coquilles St Jacques (scallops) served raw, marinaded in wine and herbs. If you don't like shellfish, the jambon de montagne is a really tasty cured Alpine ham.

For an entrée, the sole is the chef's speciality.

Cailles aux artichauts (quail with artichokes) is a real local dish. A word of warning here – caillette in the Alps does not mean little quail; it is the name of a coarsely chopped sausage made of pig's liver and herbs.

The beef of Dauphiné, though fairly scarce, is very good, and Jean-Yves, having been a chef in New York, can cook a steak just as you like it. So I go for his grilled tournedos. With steak or roasts I prefer gratin Dauphinois potatoes even to the best frites, although they are often served as a separate course. Even French recipe books like *Larousse* tell you to put Gruyère cheese in this dish, and it tastes very nice, but I have it on the authority not only of the Dauphiné Regional Tourist Board but of all the best chefs I have met here that you should not. You slice the peeled and dried potatoes thinly, add salt and pepper and crushed garlic, then cook on a very low heat until the milk is absorbed. Then you turn it into an earthenware oven dish rubbed with garlic, cover with thick cream, top with tiny knobs of butter and cook in a slow oven for over an hour, turning the heat up at the end to brown the potatoes. Delicious!

The gâteaux, often made with mountain fruits, or the famous walnuts of Grenoble, are usually good.

On the borders of Savoie and Dauphiné, a few miles from Voiron, wine growers use a local grape called Jacquère, making white wines which are not memorable but some of which have the VDQS grading for quality. Of these, Ayze produces the best sparkling wine, Apremont the best white, and if you want to try it, the Castel Anne keeps a good one at a low price. They are all a bit acidic like Gros Plante from the Loire. The hotel also keeps some good Seyssel, the sparkling version made by the Champagne method which makes a tolerable substitute for Champagne as an aperitif or in Kir Royal with cassis blackcurrant liqueur.

I still think that the rare Chignin Bergéon is the best of the Savoy whites.

For reds, the Côtes du Rhône house wine is excellent value and you can choose from a very good and long list of Rhône wines, plus a selection of good Bordeaux wines.

Château d'Urbilhac

Château d'Urbilhac
Lamastre-en-Vivarais, 07270
Ardèche (from D533 Valence
road, as you enter Lamastre,
take the little left road D2,
narrow and climbing, marked
Privas-Vernoux road).
Telephone: (75) 06.42.11.
Rooms C–F;
menus B, C, D;
half-board E per day.
Closed 1 October to 1 May.
Visa, Euro, Amex, Diners.

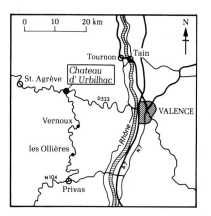

Quite a discovery for calm, rest, comfort, lovely scenery and excellent value. High in the Ardèche hills, a climbing, twisting 40km from Valence, it is a near-perfect example of a Renaissance manor house, complete with round, pointed tower and grey-green roof, but it was built by a local lawyer last century on the foundations of a genuine sixteenth-century fortified manor.

The architecture is the only fake thing about it. Most of the furniture is fine antique, with old paintings, plenty of old books, and old-style service, of which Madame Xompero is rightly proud. There are goats in the farmyard for fresh cheese and much of the food comes from the hillside farms on the vast estate. The home park alone is 150 acres and climbing the narrow, twisting drive from the road to reach the house is a bit like the old Shelsey Walsh motorcar hill-climb in Worcestershire. Barbara's Spitfire would have been more suitable than my Rover.

From the tables on the terrace, which is flanked by 1890s-style statues of women, you look down to the swimming pool, then right across the valley past farms and farmland to forests and mountains. Birds perch on the statues; red squirrels run along the walls. The Ardèche is a near-empty land and there is a lovely feeling here of having really shaken off the crowds.

Bedrooms are large and have big furniture. Mine had an enormous, high carved wooden box-bed, easy chairs, dining-size table, and a massive carved bookcase crammed with books, mostly old and leather bound. There were four tiny books of poetry by the bed. Oddly, the corner wardrobe was too small.

The panelled dining room, rich in pictures, typifies a French bourgeois dining room of the last century.

Lamastre is a pleasant, busy little town where four rivers meet, famous for crayfish and trout. Every day in June, July and August, weekends in September, Sundays in October, April and May, Le Mastrou, the most famous steam train in France, runs 33km to Tournon

Almost any way you drive from Lamastre takes you through lovely Ardèche scenery. Try driving to Vernoux, then on to the Corniche de l'Eyrieux with some fine views and panoramas, or on to Privas (56km from Lamastre), a pretty town at the foot of Mont Toulon with bright houses with round, reddish roof tiles. Historic Privas was a Protestant stronghold in the Wars of Religion – and after. Then, in 1629, the widow of its Protestant seigneur, Jacques Chambaud, married a Catholic. Privas revolted, King Louis XIII and Cardinal Richelieu led 20,000 Royal troops against its 1,600 defenders, besieged it and won. Privas is the 'capital' of marrons glacés, those superb crystallised chestnuts.

Superb walking area for the fit who can laugh at steep slopes.

through the lovely Doux gorge, climbing to 250 metres. Make sure you catch the steamer, not the diesel. Tournon has a castle (now used as law courts and a Rhône museum) with a dramatic view from the terrace over the old town, the Rhône, and on the far bank, the steeply-climbing vineyards of Tain-Hermitage where Hermitage wine is made.

Food & Drink

What a pleasure in these days of competitive inventiveness in French cuisine to find really good cooking of good, fresh local ingredients. That is what chef Didier Blachier offers, and I have thoroughly enjoyed his meals, even if gastronomic guides neglect him. He is a very good saucier, too.

The menus are all good value. On the dearest menu I had as an excellent starter bavarois de saumon – salmon pâté with a cold tomato sauce, followed by sea bass in a cream sauce dotted with caviar. For main course I chose a house speciality – noisettes d'agneau en chevreuil, which means lamb cooked like venison, in this case en croûte (in a pastry case, to keep its full flavour). The cheese-board is a delight, including Chèvre Frais (soft goat's cheese flavoured here with garlic), a beautiful farm Tome, a Viverais Picodon (small strong round goat's milk cheese) and Fourme (firm blue-veined cheese with a fruity flavour).

Among desserts is a delicious crêpes fourrées aux marrons confits – pancake stuffed with chestnut purée.

The cheapest menu was excellent value. You have four courses with a choice of three dishes on each. I started with a real country jambon de sanglier, dried raw boar's ham, which was chewy but full of flavour. I was tempted by marinaded guinea fowl.

The local trout, stuffed and baked 'en papillote' (in foil) was very succulent and fresh. My neighbour praised highly cuisse de canard fricassée (drumstick of duck, sautéed, then lightly stewed in cream sauce). There was the same delightful cheeseboard, then a choice of strawberry tart, ice cream and sorbet, or Richelieu au chocolat à la sève d'érable – a rich chocolate topped gâteau with fruit brandy – 'sève' (literally sap).

On arrival I had a refreshing dry-white Viverais housewine – a bit sharp, but fruity, which is the aim of the producers. But with my meal I drank a Croze Hermitage white at a very reasonable price and another time a dearer Hermitage Chante Alouette at 150F. This last Chapoutier wine is as full bodied as a white Burgundy, more alcoholic and generally tastes more powerful. A wine well worth trying.

The Côtes du Viverais red is not bad, either. You drink it young, and at rock-bottom price, so it is acidic. Côtes du Rhône Visan is a bargain. But I went for the 1981 St Joseph Coursodon. St Joseph vineyards, near Tournon, have only had an *appellation* since 1956, are little known even in France, and produce some of the best value wines of the Rhône, especially reds. They

have a recognizable smell, a good country robust taste and can be drunk quite young. They are not left in cask as long as Hermitage, their superior neighbours. One of the best is on this list – a Trolas made by the family of that name at St Jean-de-Muzols. Do try it. Mind you, there is also the best Hermitage red – the Jaboulet family's La Chapelle. This is a delicious wine, rich, strong and as good as any on the Rhône.

One St Joseph village, Mauves, has been sending wine to Britain for 250 years. It was on many Victorian wine lists – and the French only made it legitimate thirty years ago!

This is a sensible wine list, for knowledgeable drinkers with limited money.

Les Hospitaliers
Vieux Village, Le Poët-Laval,
26160 La Bégude de Mazenc,
Drôme (take D540 from N7 at
Montélimar towards Dieulefit;
best road to old village is left
just *before* the village inn,
then keep going upwards).
Telephone: (75) 46.22.32.
Rooms F–H;
menus B, D, E.
Closed 15 November to 1
March and Tuesdays low
season.
Visa, Euro, Amex, Diners.

The medieval knights of St John had long journeys from their ancestral homes to Jerusalem, Rhodes or Malta. The Order set up *Relais*, resting places, on route, usually fortified against brigand bands, often on hilltops. One of the safest, once you were up the steep hill, must have been the Commanderie at Le Poët-Laval. But their Relais did not have the comfort and welcome which the Morin family offer today to motorists who brave the narrow, steep climb which makes you think sometimes that you are driving over a cliff. I was totally seduced by this hotel high on a peak like an eyrie. I arrived tired and alone to a superb view, a glass of wine, and a wonderful welcome.

The rehabilitation of this derelict and abandoned village and the conversion of the later fifteenth-century Commanderie into a hotel is a masterpiece. And the view from the flowered terrace beside the superb swimming pool is truly magnificent – woods and green fields stretching right to the green and mauve hills on the horizon, like the views we used to get from slow old Tiger Moths when flying low.

You can eat on the terrace in warm weather, and it is a joy just to see the white garden tables laid with white linen clothes, fine china and cutlery, flowers, and candle lamps to be lit at dusk. Eat indoors in the light dining room and you may still see the view through the big window as you sit at a table covered with immaculate white lace cloth. The bar is large and there is a barman behind it – slightly unusual on the Continent. I was pleased and surprised by the great number of original paintings of many schools and types on the walls. Then I found that Yvon Morin was an art-dealer before he started this hotel for his son, Bernard, who is chef. Even the swimming pool is in mosaics decked with Roman slabs.

Bedrooms are modern, warm, bright, with soft cloth wall coverings and excellent bathrooms.

This was Protestant country and Poët-Laval was a Protest-

Several medieval villages, in various states of ruin, stand on hilltops above modern villages around here. Towards Montélimar on D540 is La Bégude de Mazenc, new village with old fortified medieval village high on a rock (fortified gate; old houses in alleys; some in ruins, others housing craftsmen; medieval church). Then you reach Puygiron, with its thirteenth- to sixteenth-century castle.

Montélimar is commercial, industrial and known for nougat and a twelfth- to fourteenth-century castle.

East from Le Poët-Laval (4km) is Dieulefit, prettily sited in the Jabron valley (still mostly Protestant). A pleasant country drive on D14 takes you to Grignan in Provence (28km), another town on a high rock, with narrow streets huddled under a Renaissance château, home of Madame de Grignan, daughter of the brilliant and bitchy letter-writer Madame de Sévigné, who died here in 1696.

She was buried in the little château church but in the Revolution a phrenologist stole her skull and sent it to Paris for analysis!

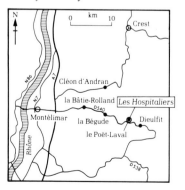

ant stronghold during the Wars of Religion and the Second Empire last century. After the Edict of Nantes promised religious freedom, the town became prosperous, known for pottery and weaving. Then Louis XIV revoked the edict and sent troops (Draggonards) to hunt down the Protestants, terrorize and destroy them. Enough stayed or returned to form a Protestant community renowned later for its Resistance units fighting the Nazis. Many who survived the Draggonards fled to Geneva, Holland or England. The village now has a museum of Protestantism (open afternoons). Potters and artisans, including weavers, have returned recently. The Knights' castle ruins include a little chapel alongside the hotel.

Young Bernard Morin, son of the house, cooks very well, uses a lot of regional dishes and is fond of herbs and spices. He cooks lobster, for instance, 'à la verveine' — with verbena, a herb I have always associated with a lemony-tasting herb tea or with a green or yellow liqueur rather like Chartreuse. Be careful, it was once a love potion. He also offers a choice of herb teas to drink with or after your meal. No, thank you — I'll take the wine.

I am told that the pricey gastronomic menu is excellent,

especially the lotte (monkfish — very popular in France) cooked in fresh ginger. The middle-priced menu is very tempting and includes in its choices some imaginative dishes such as little puffs stuffed with 'pieds de porcs' (galantine of pig's trotters) with sweetbreads in a creamy lemon sauce, and a mixed dish of fish with a thick sauce of aniseedy fennel and 'graines de pavot' — poppy seeds. He serves that lovely Bresse chicken (free range and fed on maize and buckwheat) with cucumber, truffles and a sauce of Muscat wine. Delightful.

The cheapest regional menu is excellent value. It varies with the market, as always. When I stayed, it started with a nicely varied salad of garden vegetables with a creamy, gentle local goat's cheese. Then came la caillette chaude aux herbes — a baked mixture of chopped pork, vegetables and herbs. It was very tasty. The main course was pintade (guinea fowl) — preserved in goose fat in a confit and cooked in it. The effect was excellent — guinea fowl as I have not had it before. Vegetables were excellent, too. The local cheeses were not from factories but from local farms, and my dessert was a wonderful concoction of strawberries and cream. It was a most enjoyable meal, cooked with finesse.

The service was charming, with charming Madame Morin overseeing it unobtrusively.

Yvon Morin himself is wine waiter, complete with sommelier's traditional apron and tastevin in his hand to taste each bottle and make certain it is up to standard. He obviously enjoys this role.

He has built up a very good cellar and I can read the list with delight. Many of the best wines are there. He has Côtes du Rhone and Bordeaux, from ordinaires to the best. Let him pick you a Châteauneuf du Pape. This is a wine which became popular and was stretched for quick profit. Some are still unworthy of the name. He is an expert, hand-picks the right ones and buys well. He refused to let me drink a Gigondas I had chosen. Too young, he said. Not ready. So he picked me a Chateauneuf at a medium price which was just like the old ones I used to drink years ago.

Breakfast may sound pricey but don't miss it. Fruit juice fresh squeezed from fruit, really fresh croissant, bread and cake, local jam and butter, a small fresh fruit salad, fresh green figs and an apple.

Take the right person and spoil yourself.
An hotel of finesse in one of the most spectacular positions I have ever seen.

**Hôtel Marie d'Agoult
Château d'Arpaillargues
Arpaillargues, 30700 Uzès,
Gard (4km E of Uzès on D982;
25km from A9 motorway on
D981).
Telephone: (66) 22.14.48.
Rooms and apartments E–H;
menus B (lunch only), C;
half board F–G.
Closed 15 October to 15
March.
Restaurant closed
Wednesdays out of season.
Visa, Euro.**

Leaving the lively and interesting town of Uzès, the last thing you expect to find in the unassuming old village of Arpaillargues is a truly marvellous hotel in an elegant seventeenth-century château.

You will marvel at the beauty with which this nobleman's house has been converted. Each bedroom is a delight – spacious, temperately furnished in lovely antiques, cool in summer, looking on to the garden or park. The salon, billiard room and library make me feel that Marie de Flavigny, Countess of Agoult, still lives here. I can see her sweeping down the wide staircase with iron balustrades to recieve her guests. A naughty ex-convent girl was Marie. She soon left her noble husband to live with the composer Liszt and bore him three daughters, one of whom married Wagner. Between times she wrote books under the name of Daniel Stern and had the nerve to call one *Esquisses Morales* (Moral Sketches). Ahead of her time, I suppose.

The only odd note she might find in her old home is modern furniture in the dining room, with comfortable but anachronistic chairs and tables clashing with the huge old stone fireplace – surely one of the biggest in France. In fact there is a cluster of open plan dining rooms, from this little baronial hall to an intimate little room big enough for one round table.

You can take an apéritif in the courtyard inside the gate, and in fine weather eat on a beautiful terrace by the garden. Across a lane is a lovely park of trees, lawns and flowers, with a large swimming pool. There is a hard tennis court which the French call 'le tennis quick'.

By the pool is a big bar and a barbecue for summer. In the house is a charming little bar.

The owner Gérard Savry, who also owns a delightful two-star hotel in Uzès, the D'Entraigues, is 'très gentil'.

The village was built around the château, with most buildings in the same biscuit-coloured stone in narrow streets and alleys. It would be most attractive if so many houses were not empty and derelict.

Food & Drink

I arrived late for lunch, wanting only one dish and chose assiette folle 'dégustation' just to see what was foolish about this plate. Nothing. I had a small piece of smoked salmon, smoked mackerel pâté, a good, strong chicken liver pâté and pâté de foie gras on a green salad of lettuce and endive, dotted with pieces of chicken liver, and all surrounded by slices of tomato, apple and lightly-cooked pear. With half a bottle of a local Gard wine, it was a good introduction to the cooking of the new chef, Alain Vinouze.

The card here is fairly short so that dishes can be fresh cooked, but there is enough variety for most appetites. There are some dishes with very successful innovations, like the quail pâté stuffed with foie gras, raw salmon marinaded simply in lemon and olive oil 'vierge' (not virgin in this case – first pressing!), and sea bass (bar), boned, studded with pieces of truffle, sprinkled with Noilly vermouth, then wrapped in puff pastry, and decorated to look like a fish. It is baked and served with beurre blanc (butter whipped with white wine and shallots) and slivers of truffles. The speciality starter is smoked eel mousse.

The house speciality was originally dedicated to the Duchess of Uzès in 1892 by Joseph Favre, who founded the first Academy of Cookery. Called morue fraîche à la d'Uzès, it is fresh cod marinaded with fennel, salt, pepper and myrtle, poached and served with sa-

Uzès (4km) is a delightful old town on the river Alzon. When Richelieu had its ramparts demolished to thwart Huguenot resistance beautiful boulevards replaced them. The Huguenots had destroyed the cathedral but left the remarkable twelfth-century Tour Fenestrelles, a sort of upright tower of Pisa, round, Romanesque, with six tiers of double windows. The arcaded courtyard of the eighteenth-century Hôtel de Ville leads to the Duché, château of the Dukes of Uzès. Built in the twelfth-century, it has a splendid Renaissance front. You can visit it, but not when the family are there. A market is held on Saturdays in the restored central square. Racine lived here as a young man. Museon di Rodo is a museum of early cars, motor-bikes and engines (open from Easter to All Saints' Day).

Nîmes (25km) centre of wine and silk industries, has the best preserved Roman amphi-theatre (sports stadium), with arcades and vaulted galleries, taking 20,000 spectators. Men fought lions here.

Pont du Gard (12km SE on the way to Avignon) is an aqueduct built by Agrippa in the first century BC to take water to Nîmes and is the best preserved Roman building in France. Two arched tiers of yellow stone are topped by a brick tier carrying the water. It has thirty-five arches. That bridge at Avignon (38km) is very impressive, though much rebuilt.

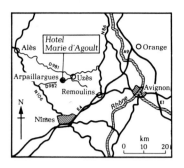

bayon (egg yolks whipped with wine), flavoured with myrtle, and topped with anchovy butter. This is a dish well worth tasting. Follow it with a delicious salad with Roquefort cheese and chopped walnuts. Then try duck in a sauce with blackcurrants or the splendid fillet of beef in Gigondas wine with bone marrow. In season you can get côtelette d'Uzès (venison chop sautéed, with cream, vinegar and orange sauce).

Among the real farm cheeses is an outstanding Chèvre de Lussan, served grilled or cold. You must try the chef's chocolate dessert with peppermint sauce.

The main menu is a four-course meal varying with seasons and market, with three choices in each course. I thought the menu outstandingly good value.

The Gard is not much known as a name among British wine drinkers, but mention Tavel rosé and most people know what you are talking about. It has a rather strong perfume, and I have known businessmen say that they only drink a nice light rosé with lunch and then order this one. In fact, it is full-bodied and alcoholic, disguised by the youthful freshness and

fruitiness. It should be drunk young before the rosé fades and it turns tawny. I am not a rosé man, but this is my favourite.

Lirac in this area produces red, rosé and white wines. A number of French producers who left Algeria operate here. Reds are usually considered superior but I had a pleasant white, surprisingly full-bodied, but not, however, in the class of the dearer white Hermitage of Jaboulet, more alcoholic than most white Burgundy.

I had also a white Château-neuf du Pape, a rarity. I like it very much – it is heavyish, like the red, and is a good sipping wine.

Gérard Savry specializes in Châteauneuf du Pape, offering a range of wines and prices, all very carefully picked, which is necessary these days for a big wine area. Appellation con-trôlée (AC) was invented here by Baron Le Roy and spread later to the wines of the nation. Red wines may be made from a mixture of thirteen grape varieties, though most producers stick to a mere nine. There is a wide quality gap between best and worst wines. Château Rayas is still regarded as the greatest. It has long wood ageing. 1978 was a superb year.

The type of wine is controlled by the amounts of different grapes used. Some is light in colour and weight (but heavy in alcohol) and is ready to drink after about three to four years. Some, as in Bordeaux, produce very good wine, matured long in the cask, which is best kept seven to eight years. Châteauneuf has the highest minimum strength of any French wine – over 12°.

le mas d'entremont

**Mas d'Entremont
13090 Aix-en-Provence (3km
from Aix on N7 towards
Celony; A7 motorway at Aix).
Telephone: (42) 23.45.32.
Rooms in house F, bungalows
in park G;
menu C;
half-board G.
Closed 1 November to 15
March; restaurant closed
Sunday evenings, Monday
lunch.**

Seductive and surprising, this dreamy old Provençal farmhouse is in a small park with views over town and countryside, hidden from the world, yet only 3km from Aix-en-Provence on the busy N7.

Creeper clad, with old solid wood posts and beams holding up the ceiling, it has been cleverly converted and furnished with elegant taste in old Provençal style.

Our bedroom, in the house, was elegantly furnished with antiques on a deep brown carpet. The walls and ceiling were covered with soft blue hessian. The original oil painting by Jean Figand was lit. A large vine grew round the balcony, and if you wished to sleep with the balcony door open there was a grill to bolt across to protect you from unwelcome lovers or burglars.

The dining room terrace is superb. It overlooks a garden pool with water lilies and fish, has a beamed ceiling, and can be enclosed with glass on cooler nights. A courtyard with a beamed roof and a fountain playing into a small pool has

chairs and tables for having aperitifs and coffee. In the garden, among lawns and rose beds, are a new tennis court and a huge swimming pool.

Aix-en-Provence – if you go sightseeing in Aix, take a bus. The traffic there is gruesome and parking very difficult.

Despite its traffic and tourists it remains one of the finest and most graceful cities in France, to me akin to Verona. Do buy a guide book locally. Its classical buildings and narrow streets harmonize with the new buildings, and the swarms of students wandering around remind you that Aix university is 500 years old and that the city was the great cultural and artistic heart of South France, and remained so until the death of Cézanne this century. Those hills rising steeply in the background were the hills he loved. My favourite spot here is his *atelier* (studio) in a house in avenue Paul Cézanne where he came to work each day from his home in rue Boulogne. It is as he left it in 1906 – simple, untidy, almost austere – the studio of a working painter.

Montagne Ste Victoire (painted often by Cézanne) – a beautiful drive (13km) from Aix along D10 to Bimont Dam in a lovely wooded site at the bottom of Ste Victoire mountain. From Les Cabassois a long hard walk up a mule track takes you to Ste Victoire Priory (built 1665) to Croix de Provence, a huge cross from below which you have a superb panorama from the Alps to the sea (allow 3½ hours for the walk). Further along the D10 is the seventeenth-century Château Vauvenargues, where the painter Picasso lived at the end of his life. He is buried in the park. Turn left on D11 to see the narrow gorge, then back to D10 and through another gorge under the 2370-foot (722-metre) Citadelle peak. Turn right on D23 to Pourrières. Here the Roman general Marius defeated the Teutons in 102 BC, slaying 100,000 men. Take the D57D past the Foreign Legion pensioners' home (Domaine Capitaine Danjou), through vineyards around Puyloubier, D57B up Mount Cengle, and D17 to Aix.

'Good King René' is another name you will meet even on cafés and shops. Exiled King of Naples and Duke of Anjou, this patron of the arts ruled Provence from Aix in the fifteenth century and started its artistic heritage. After he died, Provence was swallowed by France.

The other 'name' of Aix is less reputable. Count Mirabeau was a seducer and wastrel who was sent to prison for debt but was also a brilliant orator and, when released, joined the French Revolution, becoming representative for Aix in Les États Généraux. One of France's finest streets is named after him – Cours Mirabeau. One side is mostly cafés and restaurants, the other old town houses of the rich. Built on the ramparts, it has four fountains and lines of trees. St Saveur's cathedral of mixed styles dating from the eleventh-century has many treasures. You must ask to see them. See also the Tapestry Museum in the old Archbishops' Palace

One of Barbara's favourites – a peaceful, elegant and romantic hotel with fascinating Aix-en-Provence within walking distance.

(closed Tuesdays). And the Vasarely architectural centre 2½km WSW Aix, Ave Marcel Pagnol has geometric and colourful creations of this ultra-modern Hungarian artist (closed Tuesdays).

The menu has plenty of choice, changes a little with seasons and market, and is excellent value. I would choose it every time. On Sundays there is no card anyway.

Starters nearly always include two specialities, a spicy fish soup, and mussels with a saffron sauce. Other specialities usually on the main course are lotte farcie au pistou (monkfish with a basil stuffing), and pintadeau aux cèpes (guinea fowl with cèpes).

At one typical and excellent meal we had feuilleté d'asperges (asparagus in puff pastry casing) in a lovely creamy sauce with tiny mushrooms, followed by magret de canard (duck's breast) with sliced cooked apples in a delicious sauce of cream, cider and calvados. *Gault Millau* accused the chef of overcooking this dish, so I knew it would be right for me – *à point* (semi-rare) but not raw. The ratatouille served with it was slightly syrupy.

The basket of cheese, decorated with sprigs of rosemary, included the Provençal Banon, a lovely creamy goats' milk cheese. This one was covered in aromatic Provence herbs; sometimes they are wrapped in chestnut leaves. There was also Rigottes, another goats' milk cheese which I have eaten often in Burgundy. For dessert I chose vacherin de glace au Grand Marnier – meringue, ice cream and cream with Grand Marnier liqueur. In fact, the hotel is known for excellent pâtisseries.

Another night we started with escalopes de saumon fumé frais – thick slices of freshly smoked salmon cooked and served hot with parsley butter. It was delicious, pink in colour and tasted more like fresh than smoked.

Then came veal kidneys in a cream sauce for Barbara, dorade à l'orange for me. This is sea bream. The fish is turned in olive oil until brown, then put in a hot oven for fifteen minutes. The fish is removed, the oil thrown out, but two soup spoons of fresh olive oil are put in the same dish. One orange cut in rounds is heated in this then put on the fish. The juice of two more oranges is poured on the hot oil and reduced, then poured over the fish. It is served with croûtons of fried garlic bread.

This time we had for dessert charlotte aux fraises. It was like the Charlotte Russe we have at home, with sponge, cream and custard, but with strawberries instead of apples. The dish was invented by Marie-Antoine Carème when he was chef to the Czar in the early nineteenth-century. He was a founder of classic French cuisine. The original charlotte was a hot fruit pudding baked in a dish lined with buttered bread.

The wine list has some good Bordeaux and Burgundy wines and is strong in Beaujolais – Brouilly, Juliénas, Fleurie and Morgon, which cost a little more than the good Provençal wines. But there are some interesting Provençal wines on this list, well worth trying.

Wines of this area, Coteaux d'Aix-en-Provence, have not yet been granted appellation contrôlée, but are often as good as Côtes de Provence wines granted it in 1977. They remain VDQS (vins délimités de qualité supérieure), still closely regulated but not regarded as in AC class.

At Le-Puy-Ste-Reparde near Aix are two of the best vineyards of this area, Château Fonscolombe and Château Lacoste; the latter's wines appear on the Mas d'Entremont list and you can taste them too, at the château. We liked very much the Lacoste Blanc de Blancs, but it was not quite in the class of the Domaine du Paternel Blanc de Blancs from Cassis. Some Cassis whites are oxidized, but this certainly is not and it is interesting – the Marsanne grape gives it a body and alcoholic strength of a white Hermitage from the Rhône. Lacoste's Cuvée Lisa red is worth trying – smoother and with much more finesse than is usually associated with Provence wines. But I confess to going for the Sablet Rhône wine. We once pulled into the little village of Sablet in the Vaucluse for lunch, found it en fête and stayed two days and nights tasting enthusiastically from barrels placed around the main square. Mas d'Entremont's list is the first I have seen with a Sablet on it. It is cheap, too – cheaper than that snobby AC Gigondas from the next village in Vaucluse.

LES OISEAUX

Hôtel Les Oiseaux
Claix, 38640 Grenoble (10km
S of Grenoble by N75, right on
D269).
Telephone: (76) 98.07.74.
Rooms D;
menus A, C;
half-board D, E.
Closed November, December,
January; Friday and Saturday
lunch off-season.

True – 'Quiet Peace and Rest' motto of the Relais du Silence organisation, of which patron Pierre Vagnot is secretary

A wonderful position. Beautiful Alpine views in almost every direction. The front bedrooms look to the snow-capped Massif le Taillefer, le Grand Serre and les Alpes de Belledonne (Chamrousse, the ski resort). The back bedrooms look across to Grande Roche St Michel and Le Moucherotte. Many bedrooms have balconies for extra enjoyment of these impressive views.

A smart, white modern building, it stands above terraces of mountain stones and pretty flower beds leading down to a large swimming pool. Among the scenery and the flowers, it is a joy to eat on the terrace in good weather. It is a modern hotel with traditional French cooking. Bedrooms are fairly simple, bright and comfortable. Ours was a family room with a large bed and two singles, jolly green walls, bathroom with shower and wc (many have baths) and a large balcony looking over the garden to the mountains. Downstairs there is a bar-lounge and the restaurant opens on to a terrace.

The village is tiny, with just a post office, café-bar and three shops, though it is only 10km from Grenoble, crowded, packed with traffic and the fastest growing modern city in France.

Les Oiseaux is a superb hideaway.

Food & Drink

Avocado stuffed with shrimps, pike quenelles with a rich sharp sauce Armoricaine, trout with almonds, peppered entrecôte steak, veal escalope in a rich cream sauce, veal chasseur, tournedos Rossini (luscious centre of a fillet steak with truffles) ... isn't it wonderful to get back to the great simple old French traditional dishes?

Patron Pierre Vagnot calls it *cuisine familiale* – family cooking. And it is, even to the plate of fresh vegetables. One thing I miss most of all with Nouvelle Cuisine or most modern French cooking is being served with one little potato, two slivers of a baby carrot and

The National Park of Vercors is made up of Alpine foothills, much of it green and gentle, but climbing with frightening steepness from the Isère valley, so you must get through the outer walls. The usual route is by way of Sassenage (4km N of Grenoble), then through the Gorge d'Engins to Lans and Villard-le-Lans, a resort luring walkers, climbers and fishermen. Cable cars take you to fine viewpoints over the Vercors range and the high Dauphiné Alps eastwards. There are a dozen different routes from here, all spectacular, with gorges where waters roar in torrents and so enclosed that you find yourself looking down rather than up to the peaks. At Nizier-du-Moucherotte, there is a wonderful panorama from the Belvedere. There is also a cemetery memorial to the remarkable heroes of the Resistance who fought the Nazis from here for two years from 1942–4. The Resistance group grew to nearly 4,000 men living up in the hills and the German Army failed several times to dislodge them. Grenoble was given the Croix de Guerre in 1945. No need to go right into Grenoble from Nizier; a little road D106F off D106 leads to Claix. The whole circuit has one lovely view after another.

For Grenoble (10km) and the Monastery and mountains of Chartreuse, see entry under Castel Anne, Voiron page 133.

There was a good choice of cheese and of desserts, including old favourites freshly made – crème caramel, chocolate mousse, poire belle Hélène (cold poached pear in vanilla with ice cream and hot chocolate sauce – Helen wasn't 'belle' when I was young), café liègeois (hot coffee poured over ice cream, with whipped cream), and a good choice of non-slimmers' pâtisserie.

Wines are most reasonably priced. Some are half what more luxurious hotels in my selection charge. The Côtes du Rhône red house wine is almost at Relais Routiers price. Other very drinkable cheap wines are a 1979 Muscadet Domaine des Greniers, cheaper than the Savoie white Apremont, a Savoie red Gamay de Chantagne and a Domaine du Galet Bordeaux Supérieur. At well below average prices are Croze Hermitage red and white, a Chablis 1981, 1978 Château Gireaud – St Estèphe Bordeaux and 1975 Château de Roques St Emilion.

With my steak I paid a few francs more for a 1975 Château La Tour Blanche from Bas Medoc, north of St Estèphe. There, they make strong full wines, ideal for beef. I could not resist Muscadet at that price with the salmon. Five years old, it was smooth and, as my Yorkshire–Irish mother-in-law would say, 'wanting drinking'.

Les Oiseaux is the place for a man like me – one of the world's greatest wine consumers.

one flower of cauliflower instead of a great plate of vegetables with a spoon for digging in. French vegetable growers must be bankrupt. What is so healthy about cooking which gives you no green vegetable except a dessertspoonful of spinach?

His meals are very reasonably priced. The cheap menu offers soup, a salad according to season or a chicken terrine with hazelnuts (delicious), then duck with wine and shallot sauce, veal chasseur (cooked with vegetables) or andouillette – that coarse sausage of pigs' offal which some gourmets love and which most Britons, including myself, dislike heartily. It is strange how cheap dishes like this and stuffed goose neck, sheep's feet, cassoulet, sweetbreads, even pizza and Yorkshire pudding, invented to fill the empty bellies of the poor, have been taken up by gastronomes. Yet they despise some of the greatest dishes in the world, like fish and chips.

The 'expensive' menu costs the same as some restaurants charge for their cheapest. I had an interesting salade Dauphinoise, a green salad with tomato, orange, nuts and crab. Then I chose blinis of salmon beurre blanc – a Russian omelette filled with salmon in a sauce of butter whipped with shallots and wine. For the main course I chose entrecôte marchand de vin, rib steak with a sauce made from beef stock, réd wine and shallots, not unlike a Bordelaise. It was very good. The choice of vegetables was new potatoes or frîtes, courgettes, baby carrots and haricots verts, tiny green string beans which we usually allow to get big, stringy and tough.

Ombremont
73370 Le Bourget-du-Lac,
Savoie (2km N of Le Bourget
on N514 on shores of Le
Bourget Lake; leave A43
motorway at Chambéry exit).
Telephone: (79) 25.00.23.
Rooms G–H;
menus C, E.
Open Easter to mid-October;
restaurant closed Monday
lunch.
Visa, Euro, Amex, Diners.

Do you wish sometimes that you had decided to become a millionaire? That was how I felt as I sat taking a pre-dinner aperitif in the suntrap extension to the lounge of Ombremont, now a Relais et Châteaux hotel. It is the sort of house to which I could easily become accustomed: friends over for weekends, dinner parties, a boat on the lake . . .

It was built, in fact, for a local millionaire, then bought by an American millionaire, *the* Mr Johnston of Johnston Marine Engines. A long downhill drive away from the road, it is set on a hill with magnificent lake views across to the opposite shore south of Aix-les-Bains.

As I sipped the house aperitif (raspberry liqueur with fizzy wine), a flotilla of ducks swam an erratic course by the near shore, swallows weaved round the cypresses of the lovely terraced garden. A girl with superb legs in a sleek orange costume swam in the pool way below me. On the terrace outside the dining room just below, a family reunion was getting heartier as the drinks flowed. In the postage stamp harbour a man and a blonde girl furled the sails of the little boat they had just brought in, and stepped ashore with a small box of fish. Difficult to believe in the early-June warmth that the mountains opposite would be white and fearsome in winter.

The house is rather higgledy-piggledy, as if the owners had had afterthoughts, and it has a lot of rooms. All bedrooms except two are large, fairly luxurious and have balconies overlooking the lake. It has warmth. So has the welcome of Monique Carlo, wife of the patron-chef Pierre-Yves Carlo. They are both most helpful. He left his kitchen one morning to mend a guest's Mercedes which looked pretty but would not move.

Le Bourget Lake is the biggest in France, Le Bourget is a big village resort beneath La Dent du Chat. It has five harbours, and was for long the port for steamers which sailed up the lake to the Savières canal, then into the Rhône and on to Lyon. It is now a watersports centre

Aix-les-Bains (9km round lake) – a spa since Roman times with the inevitable casinos (why do people insist on ruining their bank balances whilst cosseting their health?). Aix is still fashionable, with lovely gardens; Fauré museum with modern paintings – Cézanne, Dégas, Pissaro, Corot, Rodin (watercolours).

The Royal Abbey of Hautecombe (15km N on N514), founded by Cistercians, became a sort of Westminster Abbey of the Duchy of Savoy, independent of France until 1860. Forty-one Savoyard princes or princesses are buried here. Since 1922 it has been occupied by Benedictines of Solesmes. Superb lakeside position. You can hear the Gregorian chant at the 9.30a.m. mass on Sundays, or in summer on weekdays, by catching a boat from Aix-les-Bains at 8.30a.m. for a special tourist service. Open for visits daily.

Chambéry (11km), capital of free Savoy until 1860, is a delightful city of narrow alleys, arcades, fine houses with turrets, courtyards and winding staircases. The fountain with four elephants in rue de Boigne is a memorial to General de Boigne who made a fortune in India and left much of it to Chambéry. The fourteenth-century castle with a massive round tower which dominates the town was the palace of the Dukes of Savoy. Chambéry produces the pale, dry vermouth that is named after it.

for swimming, sailing (including a good sailing school with holiday courses), rowing, wind surfing, water-skiing and fishing, and is the base for many motor yachts.

The eleventh-century priory is beautiful inside. The French-style formal garden, thirteenth-century carvings, fifteenth-century cloisters, doors and fireplace are all magnificent and beautifully restored. It is used now for exhibitions, conferences, reunions and wedding receptions 'at an extremely reduced cost' (Open 15 June to 15 September, afternoons.) Le Bourget's neighbour Bourdeau has a tenth-century castle.

Food & Drink

Pierre-Yves Carlo was not trained by any of the great chefs of France, like most of the well-known young cooks, but he has master touches which have earned him a deserved Michelin star. He marinades raw mullet with salmon in lime juice, makes a splendid shell-fish 'gâteau' served with cream of chives sauce, and serves a splendid mixture of lake and sea fish with dill. M. Carlo buys beautiful lake fish from local fishermen and superb fresh vegetables from local markets, and it is a pleasure to eat French vegetables in reasonable quantities again, even if not in quantities big enough to satisfy a traditional Frenchman – or me.

The cheaper five-course menu is good value and when I was there included that mixed fish dish as one of the main-course choices; the cheese was delicious Savoy mountain Tome de chèvre served hot with salad.

The six-course gastronomic menu is pricey by French standards but a great experience, First came the shellfish gâteau, then cassolette d'écrevisses au gingembre – crayfish with just enough ginger to bring out the full flavour. It was quite delicious. Next came ris de veau au vin jaune – sweetbreads cooked in the wine of Jura turned yellow in oak casks for over six years. the main course was noisette of lamb, cooked pink in the middle but not raw. I hate nearly raw lamb. The cheeseboard was excellent, with most of the delicious mountain cheeses of Savoy and fine cheeses of Franche Comté, and the pâtisserie mouthwatering.

The cuisine here is superb, but I do think the prices of some card dishes are a little steep. All right, I know about the cost of keeping up a luxury hotel like this, of a limited season, and of fresh food all freshly cooked. But we customers have our problems, too.

All the same, the dining room is nearly always full, even in April. The service, by young people, is happy and very good.

The card offers 'cocktails de tisanes' (cocktails of mixed herbs) – not for me – Barbara is our herbalist.

There are some great wines on the list up to a Château Lafite-Rothschild 1975 for 1650F, and some really good wines, like the Pernand Vergelesse Beaune and the Château Meney St Estèphe 1972 from Bordeaux at fair prices. There are some nice Savoy regional wines at reasonable prices and very fair Rhône wines.

Eighty per cent of Savoy wines are white. They are refreshing after a day's skiing but like all mountain wines can be a bit like battery acid. The wines from Jacquère grapes grown around Aix-les-Bains are nearly always acidic and are bottled from the lees, so they tend to be still fermenting slightly – *perlant*. Wines from the Roussette grape are highly rated and there is a good cheap one on this list. There is also a wine from Apremont, highly rated. But I would go for the Chignin Bergeron, a rare wine made from Roussane grape and which I believe to be best of Savoy whites. I would not bother with the Savoy reds. If you want a regional wine, try the 1976 Arbois Rouge from Jura, on the French-Swiss border. I would pick one from a bit further away – Côte du Rhône Gigondas. But it is known that I think Gigondas under-rated and excellent value. I have supped a few barrels in my day.

Its like being in Switzerland with the advantage of French prices and cooking

SOULEIAS

Hôtel Souléias
Plage de Gigaro, 83420 Croix-Valmer, Var (just inland from Bay of Cavalaire, 5km SE Croix-Valmer by D93 and a lane).
Telephone: (94) 79.61.91
Rooms H;
menu D;
half-board G, H
Closed 1 November to end February.
Visa, Amex, Diners.

You will meet the younger, fashionable set here – casual and chic.

'*Un avant-goût de Paradis*' – a foretaste of Paradise – says the publicity. Certainly in a magnificent position, overlooking the Côte d'Azur and sea, superbly run, luxurious – and very expensive.

You expect to pay for a hotel in this position on the peninsula of St Tropez. It caps a hill looking out to sea over Gigaro beach, its low buildings in modern Provençal style. Its gardens, packed with fragrant flowers, are terraced so that you have sea views from almost everywhere, especially the dining terrace outside the light and airy dining room and from around the swimming pool.

You can sip a Kir by the pool, surrounded by rosemary and pines, alongside a sunbathing topless beauty, and view the distant prospect of Île de Levant, the naturist isle where Barbara first stripped in public before total strangers and later persuaded me to do the same, thus proving that I was not the shape for it.

A five-minute walk down a path takes you to Gigaro beach.

It is a bit of a haul back. But you can drive.

Our bedroom had sliding glass doors which opened on to the pool terrace. It was huge, with white wood and cane furniture – a large settee, two armchairs, tables, and more chairs, a table and sunbed outside the window. Bedrooms in cosier country and colonial styles are in the quiet part.

Definitely a place for lounging about and doing nothing. However, there is a tennis court if you get an urge to exercise.

In the comfortable bar Philippe the pianist plays every evening in summer and weekends in winter.

Food & Drink

The chef, Eric Garcia, came from La Ferme Mougins, near Cannes, where he was praised for performing the remarkable trick of marrying traditional Provençal cooking with Nouvelle. To me, there is little Nouvelle and less Provençal about his dishes but he is an outstanding chef.

The menu, though not cheap, looks simple enough. I enjoyed my meal thoroughly. One choice of starter was terrine de rascasse sauce grelette. I could not remember what rascasse was and my dictionary said 'scorpion fish, hog fish'. Then someone mentioned bouillabaisse and it clicked – diable de mer (devil fish) essential ingredient of the great fish soup-stew. I chose instead salade Souléias. It turned out to be lettuce with sauce Roquefort and bacon and egg.

For the main course I chose pintade (guinea fowl). I often do and often regret it. Guinea fowl, like pheasant, can be tender and succulent or tough and dry, especially when badly roasted. It can also be tender but tasteless chicken in disguise in a strong sauce. This was tender, succulent and genuine guinea fowl. Cheese included a delicious, very creamy Tourrée de l'Aubier, new to us. Then came tulipe royale aux fraises – tulip-shaped meringue filled with strawberries and cream, and liqueur.

On the card his terrines are outstanding, especially duck with herbs served with chicken liver mousse, and Mediterranean fish addicts should try his pot au feu de la mer.

The wine list is good, short and pricey. I expect to pay more in a gorgeous hotel on the Côte d'Azur, but some, such as Rully, are overpriced by any standards.

However, there is a splendid local vineyard producing good Côtes de Provence AOC wines (appellation d'origine contrôlée) – cru classé (a Provence name for the better estates). There is a good choice at reasonable prices on Souléias' wine list. Domaine de la Croix, near La Croix-Valmer, is one of the most reputed vineyards of all Provence. It was started by some silk merchants from Lyon just over a hundred years ago

Gassin (5km from La Croix-Valmer) is a village 600 feet (180m) up an isolated hill left from the days of defence against Saracen pirates. Modern art in the church. From here to Cap Camaret are several fine views. See Ramatuelle, an old sloping Provençal market town with narrow alleys overhung with arcades and arches.

Maures Massif inland is a wooded chain of mountains where regular fires have often devastated the trees and main vegetation. The major industry is making bottle corks from cork oaks. Drive up to Cogolin, a village under a tower where they make the famous carpets and fabrics. You can visit the factory on weekdays. The modern marina and its surrounding modern-Provençal houses and the fine beach are 4km away. Drive on to the medieval village Grimaud named for its original owners, the Grimaldis (Prince Rainier of Monaco's family). Superb views over the Maures and St Tropez Bay. Five km away is Port Grimaud, the modern resort with canal-street, where the rich fled from St Tropez when that became too popular. From Grimaud take D538 to La Garde-Freinet, the heart of the Maures Massif. This was the great Saracen stronghold. After 732, when Charles Martel drove them back from

Poitiers, they retreated to Provence where they built forts and made raids from them to pillage the countryside. But it was not all pillaging. They brought to Provence medicine, the art of making corks, getting resin from pines, making tile floors and playing the tambourine. The ruins of their castle can be reached by a long steep walk. The reward is fine views to sea and inland.

Cavalière (21km SW of Croix-Valmer) has one of the best beaches on the coast and views to the isles of Levant and Port Cros. Cavalaire (6km) is a jolly little resort. Saint-Tropez (27km by D93 road over Col de Collebasse) may not be so fashionable these days but is as amusing and as much fun for the peasants like me who, unlike Bardot's gang, do not mind being seen out in daylight. Long ago the writer Maupassant discovered it, as a poor fishing village. Then Paul Signac, the artist, arrived in 1892 on a bike, stayed, and started a fashion for artists. Colette and her friends came next, spreading a touch of sin and glamour, and the ravers of the Twenties and Thirties, including Noel Coward and his friends, followed. Do see Signac's paintings of old St Trop in the quayside Annonclad museum, with others by Matisse, Utrillo, Rouault, Dufy and Braque. The topless girls on St Tropez's beaches are as attractive as ever.

and despite destruction during the Allied landings on this coast in the Second World War, it has long since recovered, with 250 acres of vineyards and wines which have improved out of all knowledge. Provence wines were not granted an appellation contrôlée until 1977, and there was some rubbish produced in my youth, sold in Greek amphora bottles to lure tourists.

The best La Croix wine is a red Mourvèdre, named after the grape of that name which is one of many grown and used on the Domaine. It is extensively used in making Rhône wines to give quality and ageing properties to the wine. The Croix Cabernet-Sauvignon is a bit earthier, but their ordinary cheap vin rouge has won several gold medals, including at Macon in 1982. If you like rosé, the Gris de Gris is exceptionally perfumed and soft. We liked the Blanc de Blancs, just as good as others in Provence which have a national reputation and which cost double. It has body and is fruity.

You can visit the Domaine de la Croix caves on Tuesday and Friday evenings at 5p.m. and there are tastings every day except Sunday.

INDEX OF
NAMES AND ADDRESSES

Hôtel Belle Rive 57
Au Roc du Pont, rte 039, NAJAC, 12270 Aveyron.

Hôtel Castel Anne 133
73 ave Dr Valois, 38500 VOIRON, Isère.

Hôtel de Paris et du Coq Arlequin 84
bd Dr Roux, 46400 SAINT-CÉRÉ, Lot.

Hôtel Le Calalou 124
MOISSAC-BELLEVUE, 83630 Aups, Var.

Hôtel Les Oiseaux 148
CLAIX, 38640 Grenoble, Isère.

**Hôtel Marie d'Agoult, Château
d'Arpaillargues 142**
ARPAILLARGUES, 30700 Uzés, Gard.

Hôtel Souléias 154
GIGARO, 83420 La Croix-Valmer, Var.

Hôtellerie les Champs 13
RN 138 Rouen-Alençon, 61230 GACE, Orne.

Le Logis de Beaulieu 75
ST-LAURENT-DE-COGNAC, 16100 Cognac,
Charente.

Manoir de Moëllien 19
Plonevez-Porzay, 29127 Plomodiern, Sud-Finistère.

Manoir du Stang 22
LA FORET FOUESNANT, 29133 Sud-Finistère.

Mas d'Entremont 145
Montée d'Avignon, CELONY, 13090 Aix-en-
Provence, Bouches-du-Rhône.

Moulin de Montalétang 78
MOREIL, 23400 Bourganeuf, Creuse.

Le Moulin des Pommerats 113
VENIZY, 89210 Brienon-sur-Armençon, Yonne.

Moulin d'Hauterive 109
Hameau de Chaublanc, 71350 SAINT-
GERVAIS-EN-VALLIERE (near Beaune),
Saône-et-Loire.

Moulin du Roc 81
24530 CHAMPAGNAC DE BELAIR, Dordogne.

Moulin du Vey 25
14570 CLECY, Calvados.

Ombremont 151
73300 LE-BOURGET-DU-LAC, Savoie.

Ostellerie du Vieux Pérouges 116
pl. du Tilleul, PEROUGES,
01800 Meximieux, Ain.

La Pescalerie 87
La Fontaine de la Pescalerie, 46330
CABRERETS, Lots.

Le Repaire de Kerroc'h 28
29 quai Morand, 22500 PAIMPOL, Côtes-du-Nord.

Le Saint Pierre 31
LA BOUILLE, 76530 Grand Couronne,
Seine-Maritime.

ti al lannec 34
allee de Mezo-Guen, 22560 TREBEURDEN,
Côtes-du-Nord.

Le Vieux Logis 90
TREMOLAT, 24510 Ste-Alvère, Dordogne.